GEORGE MERCER
OF THE OHIO COMPANY

A companion to *George Mercer Papers,*
edited by Lois Mulkearn,
and
The Ohio Company: Its Inner History,
by Alfred P. James.

GEORGE MERCER
OF THE OHIO COMPANY

A Study in Frustration

Alfred Procter James

UNIVERSITY OF PITTSBURGH PRESS

Library of Congress Catalog Card No. 63-21101
© Copyright University of Pittsburgh Press 1963

CONTENTS

PART I

In America, 1733—1763

Introduction

FRUSTRATION is a common feature of history and a frequent theme of literature. As found in historical records and writing, frustrations are of many kinds and on many different scales, global, international, national, regional, local and individual. Literature presents many illustrations of the kinds and scales of frustration, but the novelist and the playwright give particular attention to individual or personal frustration.

The historical biographer cannot, in the study of the lives of great men, ignore frustrations of one or more kinds and in different degrees. In some cases the frustrations are small and the great man surmounts them. But the lives of some men, not triumphantly great, reveal frustration (frequently a series or body of frustrations) as relatively complete. In the case of many such individuals the frustrations are the result of divided and often conflicting ideals, an outgrowth of variations about concepts involved in general and highly familiar terms such as men, people, country, nation, community, religion, loyalty, freedom, society, individuality and other such generalizations.

Historical biography, if sound, cannot ignore the matter of frustration. Only the fictionist, whether or not prejudiced or propagandistic, can depict a life without frustrations.

In an historical biography one must for the most part find and rely upon documents or other surviving evidence of some kind. While it is amazing how much documentation has survived and can be found and utilized, there has usually been in an individual life much which did not get recorded. This is well known to be true of the great men. Of lesser men it is even more the case. Of the so-called common men it is sometimes difficult to establish even the matter of definitive identity.

The correlation of the role of a man in his own times and of his deserved place in history is a matter of much speculative interest. Here most certainly adequate documentation plays a big role. Washington, Hamilton, Jefferson and Franklin, great in their times, left behind voluminous documentation. Their well preserved papers are invaluable not only about their own lives, but for information about many of their contemporaries.

Were it not for the extant papers of two men, George Washington and Henry Bouquet, the biography of George Mercer, a frustrated young Virginia aristocrat, could not, with any fulness, be written. It is notable that the able editor of the recently published *George Mercer Papers* (University of Pittsburgh Press, 1954), an archival work, did not include a sketch of the life of George Mercer, but in commentary and annotations provided excellent sketches of the lives of some of his associates and contemporaries.

Ancestry and Childhood

George Mercer, oldest son of John Mercer and of Catherine Mason Mercer, his first wife, was born June 23, 1733, probably at Marlborough, the family home on the Potomac River in Stafford County, Virginia. His father, John Mercer, an able, learned lawyer, who had become a planter, was born in Dublin, Ireland, though possibly of English antecedents, and with the exception of his brother, James, was without American colonial relatives, but his mother was connected with a family best featured by having in colonial Virginia no less than six successive gentlemen by the name George Mason, of whom far the most significant was George Mason of Gunston Hall, a nephew of Catherine Mason Mercer.

The relative validity, in this case, of the old axiom, "Like father, like son," requires attention to John Mercer and his home, "Marlborough." Born in 1706 he left Europe at the age of seventeen and settled in Virginia. According to his letter of January 28, 1768, to his son George, then in London, "Except my education I never got a shilling of my father's or any other relations estate; every penny I ever got has been by my own industry and with as much fatigue as most people have undergone and out of that I contributed very considerably towards the recovery of my father's estate and the settlement of my bro. James." [1] The revealing items in the statement are about education and work, both featured in surviving documentary evidence. His education in Dublin provided a remarkable and unmistakable penmanship, characterized by minute lettering and regularity of spacing of both pages and lines. It also provided interest in many aspects of culture. Not less significant was John Mercer's incessant labor, interrupted mainly, if not only, by periods of bad health so common in colonial Virginia. As his letter of January 28, 1768, clearly reveals, he established a home library of considerable size and comprehensive scope, kept up to date by new acquisitions. He consciously secured materials suitable for children of different ages. It is well known that George Mason of Gunston Hall owed much of his

8

scholarly and cultured accomplishment to the fact that as a boy and young man he lived at periods with his aunt Catherine at Marlborough. Available lists of materials on the library of John Mercer throw light not only on himself and his children, but also upon George Mason.

Before he was twenty-three years old, John Mercer had established himself in Virginia. He studied law and government, got married, acquired lands and took up the combined role of lawyer and planter.

In 1957, extensive archaeological work under the Smithsonian Institute was being carried out at Marlborough. In the process, primarily of establishing the location, foundations and size of the buildings, many hundreds of artifacts and other items have been unearthed, recorded, studied and preserved. One interesting archaeological conjecture is that the residential mansion had halls running through the structure both from front to rear and from side to side, thus dividing the main floor into four somewhat separate divisions.

It is a regional tradition and belief that life at Marlborough was on the grand scale or in high style, and at an expense beyond the income and means of its owner. Work on the plantation was done, as then usual, by slaves, under overseers and foremen. The researcher instinctively recalls other Virginia plantations, such as Mount Vernon, Gunston Hall, Stratford, Mt. Airy, and Sabine Hall.

In the case of John Mercer, to the emphasis on scholarship and culture, on the practice of law, and on the responsibilities of a planter must be added the equally typical colonial Virginia interest of building up extensive and sometimes widely scattered holdings of land, often on the wilderness frontier of that day.

Life at Marlborough was at least for John Mercer, and probably for Catherine Mercer, active and strenuous. Facilities must have been commodious, for room was required not only for a large and ever increasing family but for many and frequent guests. It is said that by his first wife, Catherine, John Mercer had ten children of whom only six survived childhood.

It was in such a home and amid such surroundings that George Mercer grew up as a boy and a young man. He had many relatives, and more friends, on similar estates in the immediate region. He belonged to the society of the Fairfaxes, the Washingtons, the Lees, the Carters, the Taylors, the Thorntons, the Corwins and others described in many regional treatises, but adequately depicted in Douglas Southall Freeman's *George Washington*. Probably as the oldest boy in the family, he accompanied his father on legal, business or social trips to Alexandria, Fredericksburg, Williamsburg and elsewhere and thereby early became familiar with the legal, governmental, business, political and social life of colonial Virginia in the middle of the eighteenth century.

Though his father, John Mercer, made jottings in large ledgers, several of which have survived, no mention was found there of George Mercer, 1733-1749. The birth, boyhood, schooling, habits, character, and other matters relating to his oldest son, found no mention in the ledgers.

Growing up on a slavery plantation, George Mercer unavoidably became familiar with the "peculiar institution" of slavery. Apart from the possibility of violent fits of temper on the part of John Mercer, slavery at Marlborough seems to have been benevolent and paternalistic. But however benevolent, the social and psychological results of such acquaintance with slavery are easily conjectured, well understood and, in the case of George Mercer, easily observed. By birth and rearing he was a member of the prevailing aristocracy in his region, the so-called barons of the Potomac and Rappahannock. That he should have acquired and maintained the ideals of his class was perfectly natural, and this seems to have been the case. Throughout his life, under circumstances whether favorable or unfavorable, he remained aristocratic in spirit and, as far as possible, in his manner of living.

Education at Marlborough

As to the early education of George Mercer, there is little doubt that it was given much personal consideration and attention by his father. But, as his neatly kept note books indicate, John Mercer was often away from home for short and sometimes for relatively long periods of time. He was therefore naturally greatly interested in tutors for his children. He probably, like Robert Carter, of Nomini Hall, had tutors for his early children by his first wife Catherine though documentary evidence of this in print or elsewhere is not easily found. Anyhow, George Mercer came to young manhood with good penmanship and with much capacity for logical organization and lucid presentation of factual matters.

On the appearance and the physique of George Mercer, information is not abundant. A small portrait of him has survived.[2] It reveals dark, well-groomed hair, deep-set eyes, regular features, and some indication of enduring immaturity. From documentary records it is evi-

10

dent that while on one hand his physique was capable of considerable endurance, facing as he did the heat of summers, the bitterness of cold winters, the fatigue of extended travel and the hardships of military campaigning, on the other hand he was sometimes sick not only for a few days, but for several weeks. In this respect he was like his father, like his brother James and not unlike his cousin George Mason and his sometime friend George Washington.

The tradition has survived, that life at Marlborough was socially gay and sportive, that much attention was given to pure bred horses and regional horse racing, that Marlborough had its own race track often frequented by other gentlemen of the region. Probably there was much feasting and drinking. Beer, ale, imported wines and probably imported rum, cognac and whisky were freely consumed. And according to custom, there were dancing and games at the races and the house parties. It was a sporting world in which young George Mercer grew into adolescence and early manhood. He was a young sport and not at all ashamed of it. Manual occupation or labor was no part of his education nor of his culture. Men of his class or status did not expect to depend upon brawn.

Education at Williamsburg

It is stated by several writers that George Mercer attended William and Mary College.[3] But destruction by fire of the early college records has rendered the institutional documentation both inadequate and questionable. One printed list of students, admittedly based on the recollections of professors, contains the names of George, James, and John Francis Mercer, all three under the date 1767. Actually, George Mercer was in the Ohio Valley in 1753, in military service, mainly, for the next ten years; and in Europe almost continuously after July 1763. Even James Mercer was thirty-two years old in 1767 and only the half-brother John Francis could have been enrolled in 1767 at the early age of nine. Since at that time colleges had academies, many sons of the aristocracy registered at an early age. It is not improbable that George Mercer entered William and Mary in 1748, at fifteen, and graduated in 1752. Extensive and intensive research would be necessary to establish the facts.

In the lack of adequate institutional data at William and Mary College, random notations in John Mercer's famous ledgers give indefinite but valuable information about George Mercer and his brothers as students in Williamsburg. The first possibly pertinent item is payment by John Mercer of a Williamsburg mercantile ac-

11

count of £ 2..7..8, November 14, 1748. The next item, found in Ledger C, is more specific, as follows: "To College of Wm and Mary, By Subscription to Schools, £ 12..3..0." This may have been a donation to the college, October 1749, but it happens to correspond to entrance fees paid April 5, 1750. Not only George Mercer at age sixteen seems to have been in college session 1749-1750, but also his brothers John Fenton Mercer and James Mercer, the last then only fourteen years old. Itemized, also in Ledger C, is settlement in October 1749 of a small mercantile account with William Prentis of Williamsburg.

On folio 131 of John Mercer's Ledger C is a comprehensive financial statement entitled "Son's Maintenance at Williamsburg Dr." The punctuation of the first word is incorrect. It should be "Sons,' " for there were three of them involved in the account. Itemized under the date, April 5, 1750, are eight transactions. The list involves "To Cash £ 1..7..6," seemingly an item from folio 119, from which also probably came seven items marked "To Do. pd" meaning "To Cash paid" as follows:

Mr. Robinson for Entrance	£ 4..12..
Mr. Grame Do	4..12..
Mr. Davenport Do	4..6..8
	1..12..6
Housekeeper	3..10..
For Candles	..15..10
For Pocket Money	3..6..4
	[£ 22..15..4]

Another item of April 1750, found in the ledger, folio 100, as "To William Dering by Lodging By my Sons Do £ 5," is restated on folio 131 as "To Mr. Dering for Board £ 5.. . . . . " Another item of April 1750, found on folio 110, "To Peter Scott, Joyner at Williamsburg By mending a table for my sons, £ ..2..6" is restated, folio 131, as "To Peter Scott for mending a Table £ ..2..6."

Put under the caption, April 5, 1750, "Sons Maintenance at Williamsburg" are several highly descriptive and revealing items, such as "To Cash pd. for Lottery Tickets" 7..10..6; "To Do. pd. for washing" 1..1..0; and four items under the general heading "To Housekeeping at Williamsburg for sundrys vizt. A featherbed and furniture £ 8.. . . . . ; A Desk £ 1..1..6; An oval table £ 1..1..," and "3 chairs 7/ £ 1..1.." a total of £ 11..3..6. Evidently the Mercer boys, George, John and James rented unfurnished rooms in Williamsburg and equipped them with the minimum essentials, but secured board elsewhere in town.

12

According to John Mercer's Ledger B, George Mercer lost his mother, Catherine Mason Mercer, June 14, 1750. It is reasonable to suppose that whether the boys were or were not then in Williamsburg, they were at Marlborough for the funeral.

It would seem from items in the ledgers of John Mercer, that George Mercer and his two brothers were in Williamsburg during July and August 1750, and that instruction at William and Mary College must have been continuous, possibly on a tutorial basis.

On folio 131, recapitulated from other entries, not found, are such items as "To general charges for sundrys vizt. To Cash pd. Mr. Preston as advanced to George £ 2..3..," "to George £ 2..3..," "to the Usher, £ 1..11..3," a total of £ 5..17..3 as of July 1750 and drawn from folio 120. Under August 1750 are three items, (1) "To Cash paid the Nurse attending Jno. and Jas. £ 2..3..," (2) "To John and James £ 1..1..6," and (3) "To Wm. Thomson for Taylors work £ 3..10..6." Since from earliest settlement at Jamestown malaria was prevalent in the area and in fact was not suppressed for three centuries, it is conjectured that the Mercer boys were afflicted by it.

From the ledgers of John Mercer it appears that not only George Mercer but also his younger brothers, John Fenton and James, were at school (presumably William and Mary) in Williamsburg at what might be called the session of 1750-1751, certainly for what could be styled the first term or semester. On September 14 is jotted down the item, "To Mr. John Holt, merchant at Williamsburg, By sons maintenance to this day [£] 4..5..7½," an item recapitulated in October 1750. In September 1750 is also mentioned an item, "To Cash to George [£] 1..1..6."

While it is not certain that the items in John Mercer's ledgers were not payments of earlier debts, it seems probable that nine items of October 1750 referring to recent or current matters, show that George and his brothers were in Williamsburg at the time. One item mentions "To Do. to Do. John James and nurse, £ 6..9..," meaning "To Cash to George, John, James and nurse." Another item says "To James Cocke, Williamsburg By sons maintenance for sundrys to this day £ 1..15..9." Another item recorded "To Richardus Covington, Williamsburg [Tavern keeper] By Georges and Jemmys Entrance to barn dance £ 2..3.. . . . ."

Recapitulated in Ledger C, folio 131, as from folio 42, is the item "To James Power for cash to George [£] 2..3.." Similarly recapitulated is an item from folio 82, "By Sons maintenance for sundries To William Prentis, merchant in Williamsburg [£] 18..1..3½" and

13

also another item "To Richard Gamble, Williamsburg By 2 wigs my sons [£] 4..6..0, By shaving them both the 1st of this mo. £ 1..1..3." A somewhat indefinite item, seemingly from folio 141, is "To Books for sundrys . . . £ 22..4..7½." The last item in this account is for £ 126..13..1½. But since there were three boys involved, it may be assumed that the educational bills of George Mercer for 1750 amounted to at least £ 40 per annum, or possibly per semester.

On the probable attendance of George Mercer at William and Mary during the winter of 1751-1752, no data have been found. The ledgers of John Mercer are often strangely blank on important matters. The testy old gentleman seems to have been greatly self centered though his love for members of his family is very certain.

The usual expenses of education are here happily documented. Included are tuition, pocket money, janitor service, lighting, room rent, board, repairs, washing, furniture, medical expenses, clothing, merchandise, dancing lessons, wigs, barber shop payments, books and lottery tickets. But items such as transportation, sports, entertainment and beverages are not found in the ledgers. Nor is there any mention of valets. The later somewhat luxurious habits of George Mercer were obviously not acquired at William and Mary.

Choice of Occupation: Lure of the West

What the aristocratic young collegian was doing in the summer and autumn of 1752 and in the winter months of 1752-1753 has not been determined. Joseph M. Toner, a great antiquarian authority, thinks he was studying law under his father. But John Mercer in 1766 implied that George was, at the time, more interested in the plumb line and the square, that is to say in architecture and surveying, than in following the practice of law. And seemingly George Mercer soon became interested in the Ohio Company and in all matters relating to the Virginia frontier. Probably both John Mercer and his oldest son hoped to find there some use of his collegiate education, particularly of mathematics and his resulting ability as a prospective surveyor and cartographer. So George Mercer turned to the west in early 1753. According to his own statement[4] on his map, he was in the Monongahela Valley in early 1753.

At a meeting of the Committee of the Ohio Company at Marlborough, February 6, 1753, an Instruction was drawn up saying, "If Colo. Cresap has not agreed with any person to clear a Road for the Company, You are with the advice and assistance of the said Colo. Cresap to agree with the proper Indians who are best acquainted with

14

the ways Immediately to cut a Road, from Wills Creek to the Fork of Mohangaly at the cheapest Rate you can for Goods and this you may mention publickly to the Indians at the Loggs Town or not as you can see Occasion." Although this item, of February 6, 1753, is annotated by John Mercer himself as "One of the Instructions given by the Comp to Mr. Gist April 28, 1752," it is not found in the three extant copies of the instructions to Gist.[5] And the annotation itself was written at least six years after February 6, 1753. It is true also that Gist was paid for the work of getting the road cut, but it is a reasonable conjecture, since Gist and Cresap in early 1753 were already along the Monongahela, that the instruction has application to George Mercer as, at the least, a messenger. Certainly George Mercer in April 1753, when winter was over and wilderness travel more pleasant, was on a mission of some kind to the Indian town, presumably Logstown, and probably to Chartiers Creek to survey and make a plot of the location of the proposed Ohio Company post, or fort, and settlement.

It may well be that the proposals of the Committee of the Ohio Company, July 25, 1753, signed by Philip Ludwell Lee, James Scott, George Mason and John Mercer,[6] were founded upon reports of his trip by young George Mercer. The ideas of the division of lands on Chartiers Creek and of the structure of the fort and the town probably came from the trained mind of the young scion of a leading member of the company. The map and its notations, of great historical importance, may be a component part of the report made by George Mercer after his return to Marlborough in the early summer of 1753. It may therefore be conjecturally dated as drawn at Marlborough in June or early July 1753, though from its provenance as a royal map in the Crown Collection, it may have been drawn up as late as 1762, for presentation to the British Government in connection with some memorial, or state of the case, of the Ohio Company. John Mercer had a copy of this map in his possession in January 1767 and claimed that George Mercer also had a copy in London.[7]

That George Mercer was along the lower Potomac on July 25, 1753, the date of a meeting of the Committee of the Ohio Company, is evidenced by his witness to the signature of Thomas Ludwell Lee to the Articles of Agreement.

George Mercer, in this his first recorded trip to the trans-Allegheny west, thus began his great acquaintance with the region. Like Washington, six months later, he probably stopped at Winchester, Wills Creek, at Gist's Place with Christopher Gist, at Turtle Creek with John Fraser and at Pine Creek with George Croghan. For a

15

whole decade his life was to be dominated by the frontier and its problems.

What the young Virginia colonial aristocrat did in the latter part of 1753 is not indicated by surviving documentation. He may have reconsidered law or surrendered himself to the mastery of surveying and cartography. But, as his father in 1768 indicated, he had become familiar with the upper Ohio Valley and doubtless remained alert to developments there.

First Military Service, 1754-1755

On the return of George Washington, in January 1754, from his famous trip of mid-winter, the situation changed with dramatic rapidity. On the basis of Washington's widely publicized report, Governor Robert Dinwiddie took steps to raise troops. George Mercer and his brother, John Fenton Mercer, entered military service. According to John Mercer, writing in the *Virginia Gazette*, September 26, 1766, George Mercer enrolled under Colonel Fry with the rank of lieutenant, and the pay of four shillings per day, February 25, 1754, at the age of twenty, and, having recruited a few men, became a part of the First Virginia Regiment, soon, on the accidental death of its first commander, to come under the command of Colonel George Washington.

Probably George Mercer was in or near Alexandria in February and March, 1754. And unless perchance he and his recruits were despatched earlier, he left Alexandria, April 2, 1754, arrived at Winchester, April 10, spent a week there and, on march again, arrived, April 20, 1754, at Job Pearsall's, near Romney, West Virginia, of today. A few days later at Wills Creek he was to hear of the disaster which had overtaken the Virginians at the Forks of the Ohio, April 17, 1754, the very day of his departure from Winchester.

At Wills Creek, in late April, George Mercer must have observed or at least sensed the prevailing uncertainty, when his almost equally young commander, George Washington, was deciding what to do, a matter treated gingerly by Freeman in his biography of Washington.

Having made his decision to advance rather than stand or retreat, Washington, after a few days work on the old Ohio Company road, moved west from Wills Creek, April 29, 1754. In very bad weather and by slow stages of advance, he reached the Great Meadows May 24, 1754. Lieutenant George Mercer may well have supervised work on the road in May 1754 just as he was to do in June 1754, June 1755, and July and August 1758. This may account in part for the fact that

16

the three companies of George Mercer, Robert Stobo and Andrew Lewis reached the Great Meadows as late as June 9, 1754.

The available records seem to indicate that George Mercer was promoted, at least to the responsibilities of a captaincy, in early June 1754. Colonel George Washington appears to have been pleased with him, for in a letter to Dinwiddie, June 12, 1754, he stated tersely, "Lieutenant George Mercer will worthily succeed to a company." [8] Possibly he was named captain, June 4, 1754, after having served as acting-captain on the march from Wills Creek. As captain, his pay per day would have been eight shillings Virginia currency, double his pay as lieutenant.

When Washington advanced from Fort Necessity on June 16, 1754, George Mercer's company marched down the mountain to Gist's plantation and he may therefore have been present at the Indian Conference, June 19, 1754. But the mouth of Redstone Creek was the primary immediate objective of Washington and marking out and clearing a road to it was a logical early step. Such work was begun June 27, 1754. According to early data, Captain Andrew Lewis with a few officers and sixty men began to clear the road, but according to a later statement of George Mercer, he himself was in command of a "Working Party" that opened up the road to within three or four miles of Redstone Creek. The men must have worked well, for on the next day the force was recalled and reached Gist's Place on June 29, 1754. In keeping with news of a strong French and Indian advance, it was time to retreat and after a frightful uphill march, in which officers' horses were used for other army purposes, the exhausted Virginians reached Fort Necessity. In the siege and battle there July 4, 1754, George Mercer conducted himself well and was wounded though not seriously. Washington after his arrival at Wills Creek entitled him "George Mercer, Cap't." On August 30, 1754, along with others, George Mercer was voted the "Thanks of this House" by the House of Burgesses. [9] He seems to have remained in the First Regiment, now reorganized under George Washington. Doubtless he found time for visits to Williamsburg, Fredericksburg, Marlborough and Alexandria. During the summer he bought at a sale in Alexandria a forfeited lot. [10]

Whatever may have been the raiment of Lieutenant (later Captain) George Mercer in early 1754, and probably it was composed of a good supply of laced shirts, braided coats, etc., after October 5, 1754, he was under the orders of Washington that "Every officer of the Virginia Regiment is, as soon as possible, to provide himself with an uniform Dress, which is to be of fine Broad Cloath: The Coat Blue, faced and cuffed with scarlet, and trimmed with Silver. The Waistcoat Scarlet, with a plain Silver Lace (if to be had) the Breeches to be blue; and every one to provide himself with a Silver-laced Hat of a Fashionable size." [11] This noteworthy change from the buckskin and coonskin of the frontier civilian and soldier, probably met with the complete approval of the young Virginia aristocrat, Captain George Mercer. It would be easy for an artist to depict any likeness of George Mercer in this prescribed garb. As stated above, only a small portrait has survived.

Service Under Braddock, 1755

Captain Mercer may have been in late 1754 at frontier posts from time to time, but in January 1755, he was at Fredericksburg with a small force of recruits for his independent company. Disciplinary trouble arose and Governor Dinwiddie suggested that they be marched to Winchester. To a complaint of Captain Mercer that his commission was unduly late, Dinwiddie cited his rapid rise in the service and advocated patience as a virtue. Mercer's recruits seem to have been carpenters, fifty of them, called at the time "Hatchet Men," or what might today be called axemen. As such the company served in the famous campaign of 1755.

With George Washington retired to private life in the winter of 1754-1755 and therefore leaving little contemporary reference, in his papers, to military matters, the account of George Mercer in early 1755 is not easily established. On May 12, 1755, at Fort Cumberland, he was attached to the Second Brigade commanded by Colonel Dunbar. His "Company of Carpenters" was an independent Virginia body and not regulars in the regular regiments. He may have been attached to Dunbar's Brigade only after the arrival of the latter at Winchester. The extant orderly books do not show that he marched from Alexandria to Winchester with Braddock's troops, but it is likely that he did march from Winchester to Fort Cumberland with Braddock's forces.

On June 4, 1755 Braddock's orders of the day required "Cap't. Mercer's Company of Carpenters to hold themselves in readiness to march at an hour's warning." [12] Probably Captain George Mercer's axemen cut down trees and hacked out shrubs on the long painful route of Braddock to Fort Necessity. On the division of the forces in early July, Captain Mercer's company seems to have been left behind at Dunbar's Camp on the mountain.[13] If, as is claimed by some, he was

18

present on the battlefield of July 9, 1755, and was wounded there, he must have accompanied Washington who, on the very eve of the famous clash, went from this Camp to the front.

Whether wounded or not, Captain George Mercer, like the more famous Colonel George Washington, soon found himself back in Fort Cumberland, and on the departure east of Dunbar's regulars, probably back in Winchester or again at Williamsburg, Fredericksburg, Marlborough and Alexandria. Both in 1754 and in 1755 his efforts, like those of Washington, ended in frustration, though not in disgrace nor in discredit.

Service Under Washington, 1755-1757

The defeat and death of Braddock, followed by the removal of Dunbar's Brigade to the Atlantic Coast, alarmed the governments of Pennsylvania, Maryland and Virginia, especially the last, for its frontier settlements extended hundreds of miles along the Alleghenies from the mouth of Wills Creek to the eastern branches of the Great Kanawha and of the Tennessee. Courageous though they were, and skillful in defense and Indian fighting, the isolated pioneers were no match for marauding bands of French and Indians who made sporadic but deadly warfare upon them. In the confusion and disaster, Governor Dinwiddie drew upon all available talent and resources. The First Virginia Regiment was reorganized with George Washington as Colonel in command. A string of small forts or posts of garrisons was stretched along the Virginia frontier. Companies of the Virginia militia under the best available officers, were stationed at these forts or posts. Washington was in general military control of such defense and travelled extensively from place to place. Among his attendants was Captain George Mercer, already acting aide-de-camp, and in September 1754 officially appointed as such. On a trip from Alexandria to Winchester, Washington, Mercer and John Kirkpatrick, a clerk, stopped at Rock Creek and surveyed a considerable stock of Ohio Company goods in storage there. These goods, probably from the fourth cargo, possibly shipped from London in 1753, were in 1756 inventoried by Christopher Gist and the inventory turned in to Washington at Winchester, and thus preserved among the Washington papers.

In late October 1755, Washington sent out a body of troops under Major Andrew Lewis, and with Captain Mercer, followed Lewis on a march toward Fort Cumberland. Three days later, they overtook Lewis encamped on the Little Cacapon. It took four days in

1755 to march in the mountains a distance easily covered in one hour today by automobile. The weather was bad in late October, but Washington was again in Winchester in early January. His return trip in deep winter may have been equally or more disagreeable. During this time "Cap't. George Mercer worked diligently as his aide and John Kirkpatrick of Alexandria as his clerk." [14]

George Mercer seems to have done double duty in the winter of 1755-1756 as aide-de-camp and messenger of George Washington and as Captain in command of the Second Company of the Virginia Regiment. When Washington in early January 1756 received orders from Major General William Shirley, Commander-in-Chief of His Majesty's Forces in North America, to march from Winchester to Fort Cumberland on March 10th, Captain Mercer and his command were not only left at Winchester but Mercer himself was sent down to Williamsburg "for more money and to satisfie how the 10,000 £ has been applied." [15] On his return he may have visited Fredericksburg, Marlborough and Alexandria. And he may not have returned to Winchester, or if he did he soon met Washington there for both of them were at Mount Vernon in early February. Washington, as is well known, was dissatisfied with the inferiority of colonial military rank when in conjunction with officers of rank in the regular forces of the Crown. Mercer had much the same feeling and a kindred point of view. This frustration of inferior rank, met in the field, Washington decided to protest in person at Headquarters in Boston.

A Notable Trip, 1756

On this first of his many long recorded trips, George Mercer rode horseback from Mount Vernon to Annapolis, thence to Philadelphia where he remained February 8-13, 1756, thence to New York where again several days were spent and then to Boston which was reached February 27th. The mission accomplished he was back in New York, March 10th for another stay of four days, and again in Philadelphia on March 17th and back again at Annapolis, March 23rd. This two month trip in the northern colonies probably influenced the later career of the young aristocrat. It may have given him a continental and possibly an imperial British point of view. And on the trip he played the role of treasurer and paymaster of expenses, keeping accounts later found in Washington's papers, accounts which indicate that the aide-de-camp himself spent money rather freely on the trip.

Again at home in Virginia in the summer of 1756, George

20

Mercer and his commander seem to have settled in Winchester as headquarters for military matters. In September, Washington received the Inventory of Ohio Company goods in storage at Rock Creek, a holograph of Christopher Gist who at this time was employed in Virginia in military and diplomatic roles. On September 7, George Mercer signed a writ of attachment against Richard Pearis.

The maintenance of discipline at Fort Loudoun (Winchester) was no small problem. Eighteen deserters were out at one time in early December. Captain Mercer was sent out in search of them. As Washington reported to Dinwiddie, December 10, 1756, "Capt. Mercer returned the 7th with sixteen of the Deserters; the other two escaped his diligence." [16] He must have had great efficiency as well as mere diligence. He probably visited many parts of the Virginia frontier of that day.

Post Commander, 1756-1757

George Mercer was put, and left, in command at Fort Loudoun, Winchester, in December 1756. As Freeman puts it, he "was directed to remain at Fort Loudoun, and to exercise particular diligence and care in the continued discipline of the men and in the further construction of the fort." [17] This was heavy responsibility and Captain Mercer was getting education in military administration and management. His instructions from Washington were elaborate and lengthy.[18] Analysed briefly, they were instructions to observe rules and orders, issue all orders for stores to be used, send to Alexandria for clothing and superintend its distribution, provide the rations of rum, expedite all expresses, watch all desertion, procure tools from below, grant no discharges, pay all the servants and pay all small bills.

On these responsibilities a new troublesome one was superimposed with the appearance in Winchester of southern Indian allies of Virginia. On April 5, 1757, Washington wrote Dinwiddie, "A letter which I received from Capt. Mercer upon my return to Alexandria informs me that 95 Catawbas . . . . are now in Winchester, waiting orders how to conduct themselves," and stating that the Indians "wanted matchcoats, shirts, leggings, and all other necessaries." [19]

According to letters of George Mercer to George Washington, April 24 and April 26, 1757,[20] the Indians soon began to "conduct themselves" very badly. The details are not recorded but the distress usual in such situations may be easily imagined. It was probably the

21

main worry of the young commandant. The old dilemma of neglect and resulting Indian displeasure versus foolish waste, seems to have been met on this occasion by the device of reasonable generosity based upon seeming necessity.

Governor Dinwiddie in early 1757 likewise found himself in a dilemma. Lord Loudoun, the new Commander-in-Chief, wanted colonial reinforcements and the use of Virginia companies in the campaign of that year in South Carolina and Georgia, but the Virginia legislators and taxpayers wanted a reduction in military expenses. In connection with the latter, Dinwiddie attempted the reorganization of the First Virginia Regiment by the reduction of the rank of some officers. On this process he wrote to Washington, May 16, 1757, "Those I have thought proper to continue are Captains Mercer . . . " etc. This, so far as Captain Mercer was concerned, was very timely, for he was almost immediately sent with his company to South Carolina. George Washington, May 24, 1757, writing from Fort Loudoun to Dinwiddie, mentions "Mr. Mercer's going off." [21] And Mercer evidently left behind at Winchester some troublesome Indian expense accounts, but Washington, after investigation of these, reported to Dinwiddie, June 12, 1757, that there was no blame to be attached, that the Indian gifts had been approved by Mercer's fellow officers. Earlier, June 10, 1757, Washington, in a letter to John Robinson, had questioned Mercer's accounts and taken measures to stop payments thereon, but he evidently quickly learned better, and on July 10, 1757 sent to Dinwiddie two receipts "for money which Capt. Mercer laid out for necessaries for the Indians," receipts which Washington earlier had shown, in Williamsburg, to Dinwiddie. This information was also, July 10, 1757, sent to John Robinson.[22]

South Carolina Episode, 1757-1758

The march of Captain Mercer's company from Winchester to Hampton and the sea voyage from Hampton to Charleston, South Carolina, are not described in the accessible printed materials.

It is known that the expedition sailed from Hampton, Virginia, May 31, 1757, and "After a long passage . . . arrived safe" at Charleston, June 15, 1757.[23] It is also known from the voluminous correspondence of Colonel Henry Bouquet, in command of the expedition, that there was smallpox among the Virginians and that many were infected by the disease. According to Bouquet the climate was not salubrious and the heat was almost unbearable. He also was caustic about the billets and quarters available for his troops.

22

In a letter of August 17, 1757, from Charleston, to George Washington, Captain Mercer stated, "I wrote you via Philadelphia, a few days after my Arrival," [24] but this first letter probably of late June, has not been found. In this second letter, he praises Colonel Henry Bouquet, his new commander, and writes much about Charleston, which he found a small place, its inhabitants overrated, its young ladies not beautiful, the local gossip often scandalous and the "Shape of the Ladies" not good. But he praised highly the reception and treatment given him and the Virginia troops, probably, however, having in mind the officers rather than the privates.

Possibly the climate of South Carolina in August was too much for Captain Mercer, for, on August 26, 1757, writing to Governor Henry Ellis of Georgia, Bouquet said, "I send you one Company of the Provincial Troops of Virginia, as you have desired," "Capt. Mercer being sick, Lieut. Stuart hath the Command of the Same." [25]

Evidently the sickness of Captain Mercer was long drawn out. He probably had malaria which was almost chronic along the southern seaboard. But he was able to write, November 2, 1757, to George Washington, stating, "We have still hoped to see Virginia this Fall, till the Arrival of a Man of War, from Lord Loudoun," adding such remarks as "I find my long stay in this place has only increased the very bad opinion I at first conceived of it" and "were I safe at Home So. Carolina would be the Last Place I ever would come to." [26] Ten days later, November 12, 1757, Colonel Bouquet wrote Governor Henry Ellis, "I have orders from Ld. Loudoun to send back to Virginia the Troops of that Province . . . Capt. Mercer who will have the honour to deliver this Letter, has been detained here by sickness. I take the Liberty to recommend him to you." [27] Nearly a month later, Colonel Bouquet in another letter to Governor Ellis, December 10, 1757, wrote, "Captain Mercer arrived here yesterday with his Company, he expresses the utmost Satisfaction of your Goodness to them and in general of the kind usage they have met with in your province." [28] Evidently George Mercer returned to Virginia in mid-winter. Bouquet himself was soon ordered to join the proposed campaign of General John Forbes directed against Fort Duquesne. One of the important results of this Carolina episode was that in addition to more extended travel and despite unfortunate illness, George Mercer had won an acquaintance and an enduring friendship with Colonel Henry Bouquet, a significant figure in the history of the colonial frontier from 1758 to 1764. The loss of this friendship, by the untimely death of Bouquet in 1765, may be considered one of many frustrations in the life and career of George Mercer.

In the Second Virginia Regiment, 1758

The British imperial officials, political and military, called for the greatest possible colonial assistance for the projected campaigns of 1758 against Louisbourg, Ticonderoga and Fort Duquesne. Virginia responded to the call by the establishment of the Second Virginia Regiment, whose command was assigned to Colonel William Byrd III, of Westover. The new commander probably knew Captain George Mercer and his influential relatives and he needed an officer with the experience of George Mercer. Colonel Byrd, therefore, offered Captain Mercer the position of Lieutenant Colonel of the Second Virginia Regiment. Since like another Virginian, a more famous George, Captain Mercer was ambitious, he quickly accepted the position which incidentally carried payment of half a guinea per day. And evidently he threw himself and his influence into the scales in promoting the interests as well as the organization of the new regiment. And since Colonel Byrd was absent bringing up southern Indians to the support of General Forbes and did not reach Winchester until the last of May, the organization and establishment of the Second Regiment must have fallen mainly upon Lieutenant Colonel George Mercer.

Obviously, and not unnaturally, Colonel Washington, his earlier patron, was none too well pleased. On April 24, 1758 he wrote to John Blair, the influential Virginia politician, "That was a most extraordinary request of Colonel Mercer's concerning the exchange of officers, and calculated it would seem rather to breed confusion and to gratify his own vanity than to benefit the other regiment." [29] Washington, fully aware of his own ambition, but never seeing it as vanity, was possibly entirely correct about Lieutenant Colonel Mercer. And this action of George Mercer may have, for a time, cost him the favor, support and patronage of the man destined to dominate the American scene in the last quarter of the eighteenth century. That Mercer did not lose entirely the friendship of Washington, was highly creditable to both.

Lieutenant Colonel Mercer seems to have proposed to gather a "Troop of Light Horse" in the Second Regiment. This is mentioned without comment, favorable or unfavorable, by Washington in an order to a friend, May 24, 1758.[30] He may have been displeased or amused, but he may have been merely indifferent or possibly have welcomed this innovation, later made famous by Henry Lee (Light Horse Harry) and imitated by John Francis Mercer in 1781 at a critical stage in the Revolutionary War in Virginia.

24

Colonel George Mercer was at Winchester in early June 1758. There he was chief officer under Colonel William Byrd III, who as the junior of Colonel Washington was in turn under Washington, while both regimental commanders were subject to orders from Colonel John St. Clair, Deputy Quartermaster-General. On June 9, 1758, St. Clair wrote Colonel Bouquet, " . . . Lieut. Col. Mercer shall join you after the Ten Companies wt. ye Indians are set off for Fort Cumberland." [31] Four days later St. Clair issued orders that "Col. Byrd with as many Companies as are ready of his Regiment to march the 26th" and "the Rest of that Regiment to follow with Lieut. Col. Mercer as soon as they can be got ready." [32] Getting ready evidently took little time for at the beginning of the second week of July 1758, Colonel Byrd had his regiment in rendezvous at Fort Cumberland, from which, July 9, 1758, he wrote Colonel Bouquet, "Col. Mercer marches tomorrow with two other Companys of mine and one of Col. Washington's Regiment," adding, "I take the Liberty to intreat you Sir to send him back to me as soon as he has open'd the Communication, for he is of great Service here." [33] Obviously George Mercer had won another advocate and friend, though the later collapse of the military and political status of Byrd was to be yet another frustration of his fellow officer and fellow aristocrat. On the same day Colonel Washington notified Bouquet, "Three Companies under Colo. Mercer proceed on the Raystown Road, which we began to open yesterday." [34] Unlike Byrd, Washington does not plead the need of the service, at Fort Cumberland, of his onetime aide-de-camp. The reaction and reply of Bouquet was immediate. He wrote Washington, July 11, 1758, from "Reas Town," "We begin tomorrow to cut the road on this side to meet Col. Mercer and save him the trouble of going so far." [35]

On this road building assignment of mid-July 1758, Lieutenant Colonel Mercer was not blessed with good fortune. His supplies from Fort Cumberland began quickly to run short. He wrote Washington, July 12, 1758, "I had a most violent fit of the ague and fever Tuesday, which confined me all day, from 8 in the morning to a waggon and did not leave me till the same hour next morning." [36] To those familiar with malaria it is obvious that this was probably a recurrence of his sickness at Charleston just one year earlier. But the conscientious and determined young officer also wrote, "If I have my health dont doubt but I will be very diligent in completing the road, but I assure you 2 or 3 more fits will make me incapable of anything." [37] Washington informed Bouquet the following day, July 13, 1758, "By a party from Colo Mercer, to this place for Provisions, I find they have open'd the Road 6 miles only." [38] A part of the blame Washington thought was due to the unnecessary 30 foot width of the road then being constructed. Sickness, shortage of supplies and hostile Indian attack, actual or threatened, may have slowed down road construction; but within two weeks with forces working both from Fort Cumberland and Raystown the communication between the two posts was opened up, before anything more than explorations and surveys had been made of the road from Raystown to Loyal Hannon. It was on July 27, 1758, that Bouquet wrote Washington, "Lt. Col. Mercer tells me that the Second Regt. will want about 12 Tents in all." [39] The Second Regiment, of 859 men, was at Fort Cumberland in early August. Presumably Lieutenant Colonel Mercer was there with them. A month later he was at Raystown for Washington addressed him there, September 9, 1758, saying only three days' flour remained at Fort Cumberland, and requesting Mercer to facilitate and expedite the transmission of supplies from Bedford to Wills Creek,[40] an interesting matter in the light of Washington's famous effort to have General Forbes follow the older road used earlier by Braddock.

By the end of July 1758, the Indians brought up with so much trouble from the South, had sneaked away and gone home. The Virginia forces were drawn out from Fort Cumberland and engaged in defending communications against hostile Indians and in working upon Forbes Road. Early in September some of the British forces marched across two ridges of mountains and descended upon Loyal Hannon, an old Indian town along the upper Loyalhanna. Work on a fort there was immediately begun. Gradually assembled in or around this fort were companies of British regulars as well as of Pennsylvania and Virginia colonial troops. The episode of Grant's expedition and defeat in late September was an important interlude. And equally important was a French and Indian counterattack upon the post of Colonel James Burd at Loyal Hannon. Meanwhile the Second Virginia Regiment was along the lines of communication. Lieutenant Colonel Mercer was Field Officer of the Day, September 22, 28, and October 2, 6, 8, 22 and 24. The regiment reached Loyal Hannon in the last week of October and Lieutenant Colonel Mercer was Field Officer for the Grass Guard, November 9, 1758.[41]

At Loyal Hannon the weather was bad, winter had set in, the pay and enlistment of several thousand colonial troops were due to cease at the end of November and General Forbes was gravely ill. The situation seemed desperate in the second week of the month. Then it changed suddenly, with dramatic results.

26

Rumors of an impending enemy attack, probably aimed at the destruction of the horses and cattle of the encampment, led to a British-American attempt to surround and capture the supposedly approaching enemy. About half a regiment of Virginia colonial troops (presumably from the First Virginia Regiment) were sent forward under Colonel George Washington in one surrounding movement and a similar body (presumably from the Second Virginia Regiment) under Lieutenant Colonel George Mercer was ordered to complete the surrounding movement. It happened that these two forces on approaching each other mistook allies for enemies and opened fire, with loss of 14 killed and 25 wounded before the firing could be halted. Thomas Branon, a sergeant in the command of Lieutenant Colonel Mercer, later petitioned the House of Burgesses for recompense for being wounded "in the Neck," on the 14th of November.[42]

A fortunate circumstance of this warfare in the woods was that a few of the enemy were captured and, under pressure, revealed that the French, because of inadequate provisions, were withdrawing from Fort Duquesne.

On a slight improvement in the now wintry weather and with the necessary courage for at least one last attempt to reach his first goal, General Forbes ordered a general advance of his army. In this advance Lieutenant Colonel George Mercer, with the Second Virginia Regiment, was in the division under Colonel Montgomery. He was Field Officer at Turtle Creek, November 21, was in command of some forces November 22 and 23, 1758, and doubtless marched with them into the smoking ruins of Fort Duquesne.[43]

In about ten days General Forbes had marched from Loyal Hannon to Fort Duquesne, but he himself was desperately ill. Indian affairs were critical, shelter was lacking, supplies were dangerously low and only a small fraction of his troops could be kept for any length of time at Pittsburgh. He quickly decided to march his British regulars east to winter quarters. And, as Forbes wrote General Abercromby, November 26, 1758, "The Pennsylvania, Maryland, Virginia and North Carolina troops may all disband tomorrow, as their provinces pay them no longer." [44]

It seems that the bulk of the Virginia troops left the Forks of the Ohio immediately after its capture. Presumably they went back along Forbes Road to Loyal Hannon (first re-named Pittsburgh and, later, Ligonier) and on to Raystown (re-named Bedford), and there, parting with the British regulars, turned south to Fort Cumberland, with many going on to Winchester and eventually to their homes and families.

27

Colonel William Byrd's Second Virginia Regiment lost its field organization and probably, temporarily, its establishment. Colonel George Mercer returned home and was in Williamsburg late in January. Governor Francis Fauquier wrote Colonel Byrd, January 23, 1759, about rebuilding the regiment, saying about proposed new officers, "Lieutenant Colo Mercer who will deliver this to you, can give you a better Acct as they are mostly his Friends, so he may know their Dispositions," and adding, "I am not without hopes of reinstating him, but this Affair in Embryo." [45]

Imperial Recognition and Status, 1759

But Lieutenant Colonel Mercer had the good will of Colonel Henry Bouquet and the latter probably recommended him to General John Stanwix who had succeeded General Forbes as commander in the southern department. Evidence seems to indicate that General Stanwix summoned Lieutenant Colonel Mercer to meet him on the coast, possibly at Philadelphia. Probably as a result of this George Mercer was in Philadelphia in late March and early April 1759. He may have received promises of appointment and promotion from Stanwix, which in turn may have needed confirmation from General Amherst. As yet the status of Mercer appeared indeterminate. But he, on his way back to Virginia, stopped at Annapolis, where on April 17, 1759, Governor Sharpe in a letter to the proprietor, mentions "Lieut Colo Mercer of the Virginia Forces who is just come from Phiadelphia." [46] Very probably Mercer spent the summer of 1759 in military service. In early August he was ordered to push the clearing of Braddock's Road, a matter demanded both by the interests of Virginia, and by the necessity of forwarding supplies from Maryland and Virginia to the military forces and laborers then being assembled at Pittsburgh. About his somewhat indefinite and also anomalous situation George Mercer wrote General Stanwix, August 12, 1759, saying he was serving as a Volunteer "being even out of Commission from the Colony." [47]

One week later, August 19, 1759, he was granted a warrant appointing him Assistant Deputy Quartermaster-General for the provinces of Maryland and Virginia,[48] a position corresponding to that of his intimate Friend, Captain Lewis Ourry, in Pennsylvania. While the warrant was sent to Mercer by Colonel Bouquet, the appointment was made by General Stanwix then at Bedford en route to Pittsburgh to superintend the construction of a powerful new fort. In his letter of notification, Colonel Bouquet, on the authority of Stanwix, outlined the nature of Mercer's work and the pay received in such a position. The compensation of "Seven Shillings and Six Pence St. per day during the time employed" was insufficient for the living expenses of one with the habits and outlook of Lieutenant Colonel George Mercer, a situation not helped by the fact that in connection with his functions he was assigned a "Credit for Eight hundred Pounds Sterl. upon Col. Hunter," the Virginia Paymaster.[49]

Thus began what was possibly the most important service and successful effort in the half century life of the young colonial aristocrat. His rank and authority may not have been high and his pay was small, but his duties were manifold and his responsibilities heavy. Roads, wagons, horses, boats, barrels, convoys, as well as tents and clothing, were involved. But contracts for provisions, prices, accounts, payments and settlements of accounts were also a part of his obligation. In many ways he was a combination of quartermaster, commissary and paymaster. His correspondence with Bouquet at this period is burdened with problems and detail. His major responsibility was that of opening and keeping cleared Braddock's road from Winchester to the Monongahela Valley. A feature of this was providing supplies for Colonel James Burd in his construction of the road to the mouth of Redstone Creek in 1759, work which Washington, Lewis and Mercer had first started in June 1754. Colonel Bouquet mentions "Col. Mercer having agreed with Col. Burd in August last to supply him upon the Monongahela with Provisions from Virginia." [50] Fort Cumberland seems to have been the geographical key, but Winchester was hardly less important. Mercer found Fort Cumberland in great need of repairs in August 1759. He found himself with no carpenters and no tools. He proposed to go at once to Winchester to secure them.[51] He travelled widely over Frederick County, Virginia. Conditions since 1753 had improved but as yet very little. His letters claim that the settlers were unreliable and sharp in business matters. Vexation on his part may account for some of his unfavorable comment. "The old misers," he wrote, "take more delight in telling over the Pieces of Gold or Silver than twice the Quantity of Paper." "Pray Sir," he wrote, "be pleased if possible to send me down some Gold or Dollars," for, he added, "it will have a strange Effect upon the Eyes, and Minds, indeed, of the Farmers." It is not impossible that he himself realized fully the difference between British pounds sterling and colonial paper money. The lack of cash and the extent of the use of credit and of resulting indebtedness were familiar to Colonel Mercer and most of his contemporaries. Financial frustration and unfortunate

29

decisions, based upon or caused by such frustration, increasingly dominated his later years.

At Fort Cumberland, Colonel George Mercer, A.D.Q.M.G., saw quickly the advisability of promoting water transportation along the upper Potomac. He knew about or had heard of old scows formerly in use but later stranded and lost sight of. Probably these old scows had been used by the Ohio Company, 1750-1755, and possibly by Braddock. Mercer proposed to find them along the river and restore them to use or, as an alternative, build new ones. Mercer wrote Bouquet that artificers, especially those capable of building a scow, were very scarce and very expensive at Wills Creek.[52] In a letter to Colonel James Burd, September 1, Colonel Bouquet explained transportation and supply difficulties, saying, "Mercer writes me that he wants a Ship Carpenter to Cork [sic] the Scows upon Potowmack."[53] Colonel Mercer, as was well known by Colonel Bouquet, showed great interest in promoting trade of Virginians with the Ohio Valley. He tried to incite individuals to enter upon the trade, and probably after two full years of association with George Mercer the alert Bouquet knew much about the Ohio Company and George Mercer's relation thereto.

Bouquet preserved, for himself and posterity, six letters from Mercer in the month between August 28 and September 28, 1759. The matter of the old scows got repeated mention. That after much search they could not be found is little surprising. In his long letter of September 28, 1759, Mercer discussed a crooked deal he suffered in saddles for pack-horses. He reported a bad drouth which dried up most of the mill streams and shut off much of the production of flour, and he portrayed the incessant problem of prices and payments. He strongly stated his desire to be in Williamsburg in November, on private business "of the greatest importance."[54]

The letter, September 16, 1759, of Lieutenant Colonel Mercer to his old companion-at-arms, George Washington, was newsy and has been much used by later historians. Mercer said he had not been east of the Blue Ridge since June. He informed Washington about his plan to be in Williamsburg in November, though he, in propriety, omitted the Mercer family financial crisis revealed in the now accessible George Mercer papers, and used his military land claims as the object of his trip, stating that he had intended to go to England itself in 1759. He naturally reported his new commission from Stanwix and informed Washington, "We are going to build a very respectable Fort at Pittsburg, of Bricks,"[55] leaving to posterity the uncertainty of the word "We," as used.

30

The situation and particularly the perplexities of George Mercer during the month of October 1759, are clearly revealed in surviving correspondence. In a letter, mainly about supplies, Bouquet, October 1, 1759, promised Mercer, "I shall mention to the General that your private affairs call you to Williamsburg the beginning of Novemr. and there will be no difficulty to obtain his leave persuaded that you will come up again as soon as you can." [56] Mercer at this time was accused by Thomas Barrow, at Pittsburgh, of having "been a little perplexed with notions of exchange." [57] The Assistant Deputy Quartermaster-General was reprimanded by Bouquet for having bought beeves (on "my Orders") probably in excess number and of inferior weight and quality,[58] a matter which Mercer admitted in his letter to Bouquet, October 9, 1759, a letter in which Mercer again stated, "I must again, as my Business is very urgent, repeat my Request for leave to go to Wmburg." [59]

George Mercer's letter of October 4, 1759, to James Burd, on Redstone Creek, is of much personal biographical significance. It says at the end, "I have a dull Time of it — No Amusement, but much business and in case of an idle Hour which very seldom happens, I am obliged to betake myself to a Book for Conversation as this Town does not abound with good Company, indeed it has none and I am the only creature here that struts militantly or appears with Scarlet or a Sword Knot so that I really appear by myself." [60]

The correspondence of the middle of the month is largely about supplies, particularly for Colonel Burd's construction forces, a matter in which Bouquet continued to manifest great interest.[61] And when Mercer, from Winchester, blamed Joseph Galbraith at Fort Cumberland for lengthy inspections of goods in transit to the Monongahela, he got in answer a sharp rebuttal of the allegation.[62]

Probably the most important and certainly the most self-revealing biographical information on George Mercer is that found in his long letter of October 27, 1759, to his trusted commander and friend, Colonel Bouquet.[63]

Several matters are dealt with, each of importance then and later. He repeated the more than a month old request for temporary leave from his post and duties that he might go to Williamsburg about a private matter that probably meant £ 500 consideration to him. Probably in relation to the necessity of this, he detailed his situation in his assignment. His hours were long, his duties heavy and the result was excessive fatigue. In addition his expenses were high and his pay inadequate. He claimed his bare living expenses amounted to seven shillings sixpence per day. High rent for his room was an item and he mentioned the "two Servts and the Horses I am obliged to keep." Since he was no longer on the Virginia payroll, he wondered, so he said, if better pay in a better position in the British army could not be secured for him. Much of this has the appearance of emotional frustration. Attempted self-analysis and revelation appear in his statement "I thank God, I am blessed with a Sufficiency to live well and genteely on, never more than since you have known me. As I despise Money farther than to answer the common uses of well living, I never coveted more." [64] The matter of living less well is expressed, but blandly rejected. It may well be that this was a critical moment in his life. More than one Virginian of the planter aristocracy had the same outlook and took a gambler's chance on the future.

On the same day, October 27, 1759, Colonel Mercer wrote to General John Stanwix at Pittsburgh. He discussed supplies, recommended Mr. Graham as contractor for such supplies, assumed himself the responsibility for sending up large amounts of "Cheese Butter," and, asserting his wish to go to Williamsburg about "a Law Affair," announced that in order to take care of it he must set out the following day, which he was certain would cause no trouble for he had affairs well in hand and he would return quickly.[65]

The trip of Colonel Mercer from Winchester to the Virginia seaboard probably took place in late October and early November. On his return to Winchester he wrote Colonel Bouquet November 28, 1759, "I received yours of the 9th Instant on my Return from Williamsburg, where not only my Business, but a most violent Cold I had taken detained Me many Days longer than I expected." [66]

The exact "Business" or "Law Affair" of George Mercer in Williamsburg in November 1759 is not definitively certain. It may have been in connection with land claims under the Dinwiddie Proclamation of February 19, 1754. But it seems also to have included or been in connection with a land release, involving a deed of large tracts of land from John Mercer to George Mercer and James Mercer, a penal bond to John Mercer for the sum of £ 6000 from George Mercer, James Mercer, John Tayloe and Presley Thornton, and a release of the tracts of land mentioned in the deed, by George Mercer and James Mercer to John Tayloe and Presley Thornton.[67]

Since the release, in the handwriting of John Mercer, was found in the George Mercer papers, and not found recorded anywhere, it has the appearance of a complicated system of mortgage by which John Mercer secured money for his heavy debts and his sons received

32

claims to vast tracts of mortgaged land. From the document itself certain data about George Mercer can be gleaned. He was in Virginia, possibly at Williamsburg, with John Tayloe, Presley Thornton and James Mercer on November 5, 1759. He was still in Virginia on November 25, 1759, the date of the signatures upon the land release. And, as noted earlier, he was back at Winchester upon his duties, November 28, 1759. Where the signing was done is uncertain though it was probably done at Williamsburg. If so, George Mercer made high speed, for that day, in getting to Winchester within three days. In the meantime, he continued his interest in "our Scow." [68]

While in Williamsburg promoting legislation to secure promised military bounty lands, George Mercer may have submitted himself to the authorities as a surveyor of such lands. On December 10, 1759, he was duly appointed as an authorized surveyor.[69] His limited correspondence of December 1759 was in relation to supplies of salt and other necessities of military provisions. Seemingly he had a visit from Colonel Bouquet during the month. Since Bouquet possessed lands in nearby Maryland, the visit may have been social as well as official.

The life of George Mercer in January 1760 is dramatically stated in his letter of January 25, 1760, to Colonel Bouquet. Neither abstract nor paraphrase would do it justice. The biographical part of it is: "Since you left me I believe no man ever felt more cruel Fortune than myself. A Gentleman of the physical Tribe prescribing drawing of a Tooth, as the surest Cure for the Pain, broke the Tooth, and at the same Stroke was so extreamly lucky as to fracture my Jaw Bone which for twenty odd Days made me delerious, frantic, raving mad, nay if I coud say any Thing worse of myself, I am convinced I have a very just right to do it, but thank God, I have at last got the better of it." [70]

In midwinter, in that day, military matters were usually quiet. The roads were bad and ordinary transportation difficult if not impossible. In this relative inactivity, George Mercer, in addition to care for his healing jawbone, seems to have worked upon his financial military accounts and reflected upon his military land claims. In connection with the latter, he expected trouble with a rival faction and its surveyor, Thomas Bullit, and wrote a letter to George Washington, the dominant figure and worker in the matter of bounty lands. This letter of February 17, 1760, frequently cited in footnotes, definitely represented reestablished relationship of Mercer with Washington. In the letter George Mercer announced, "My Business calls Me to Phila.," [71] meaning thereby his military accounts.

33

At Winchester in February 1760, Colonel Mercer found " . . . the Town and Country around Us being much infested with the Small Pox, which has now become fatal," as he wrote Colonel Bouquet, March 1, 1760, saying also, "I have waited your Orders to repair to Philadelphia with great Impatience for some weeks past . . . " [72]

On the life of Colonel Mercer in March and April 1760 information is slight. Presumably he stayed on at Winchester in the routine of his position. And in May he put in a claim of £ 266.0.6. for a share in the sale of land bought by George Washington, a claim recognized and paid by Washington.[73] In May he was in Philadelphia settling accounts with Bouquet and eventually with General Amherst. On May 24 he signed a document saying, "Received from Colo. Henry Bouquet the Accounts of Ballances due the People of Virginia which together with Mr. Walkers own General Account I am to deliver to said Mr. Walker, at Winchester, he being appointed to pay the same." [74] But seemingly George Mercer took much time in reaching Winchester. He saw Governor Sharpe of Maryland on the trip and carried letters from him to Governor Fauquier at Williamsburg in mid-June.[75] He presumably was at Winchester in late June and he may have been in Frederick County during the mid-summer months, for he now had a plantation on the Shenandoah River. But in October 1760 he was again in Williamsburg from which he went to Fredericksburg.[76] Late in December he was again in Philadelphia for he wrote Bouquet, December 27, 1760, a letter of importance for his biography. He featured the long letter with the statement "I have only been in Town two nights, and as you know I am no Swainer, have not made a single Tea Visit yet, nor am I certain I shall." [77]

Thomas Cresap had earlier asked Colonel Bouquet to become a member of the Ohio Company,[78] and now in this letter George Mercer enlarged upon the idea. He hoped to see Bouquet and said, "I shall let you see all the Papers etc. relative to the Company Business," an exaggeration or at least a careless use of the word "all," for by this time the papers of the Ohio Company were voluminous and it is doubtful that its books were sent to Philadelphia. He may have had copies of the more significant documents, some of which copies may have remained in his possession and thereby became a part of the now well-known George Mercer papers.

In this letter Colonel Mercer stated, "I shall be here and at New York till the middle of February."

From this somewhat scanty record it is apparent that George Mercer in 1760 had declined the "Honor" of continuing as Assistant

Deputy Quartermaster-General in Maryland and Virginia, possibly in June 1760, but almost certainly before October and had turned to such activities as: settling old military accounts, such as those of the expenses of Virginia in connection with recruiting southern Indians under William Byrd III, Richard Pearis and others; establishing his own plantation in Frederick County, Virginia, acting as scout and agent of the Ohio Company in which, by the unrecorded deed of his father, he had a half claim to a one-fortieth share; and finally in entering politics as a candidate with George Washington for the two seats, from Frederick County, in the House of Burgesses.

Political Adventure, 1760-1763

Mercer was well and widely known in Frederick County. On his military service and his duties as Assistant Deputy Quartermaster-General he had ridden into probably every section of the county. He now probably retraced his earlier trips. Possibly March and April were spent in such action. According to Freeman's *Washington* (III, 62), "George Mercer canvassing actively, had spent [before the election of May 18, 1760] approximately £ 50 on account of his fellow candidate." He adds, "Washington repaid him in cash on the day after the election" (Washington's Ledger A, folio 40). Here, George Mercer met with success rather than frustration. His father, John Mercer, evidently was in Winchester on election day for he mentions the outcome in his ledger. For the time Washington, Mercer and James Wood, founder of Winchester and clerk of the court of the county, were the three powerful political figures in Frederick County.

It is claimed that Lieutenant Colonel George Mercer was given a colonelcy in July 1761[79] but where and why is not apparent. George Mercer himself stated his situation in a letter to Bouquet July 25, 1761, as follows: "Since I left Phila. I have been up and down so often in the World, frequently sick, indeed seldom well, out of Spirits, fretting and Confused, that I never had an Opportunity of writing you and I really am now so much indisposed, that had I not some Business of Consequence I should not have troubled you." At the end, he wrote, "do Me your Friend the Favor to Write Me as soon as possible to Philadelphia for which place I set off next week." [80] About two weeks later, in his letter of August 9, 1761 to Bouquet he said, "My Ill state of Health, has kept Me here longer than I intended, but tomorrow I certainly set off for Phila. where I shall be glad to receive your Commands." [81] Without giving the reasons, Mercer reported that he expected to continue the trip from Philadelphia to

35

New York, Halifax and Louisburg. No mention by him of such a trip to Louisburg appears in any of his correspondence. It is faintly possible that like others, he thought a sea voyage would be beneficial to his health. But probably the projected trip was in connection with a claim of £ 1,100 by John Mercer against one Samuel Wroughton, who had lived at Marlborough as a guest for three years, and finally made arrangements to pay £ 300 on account, but had kept possession of it, and departed clandestinely for Louisburg, leaving behind £ 800 of debt which had to be paid by his host, a claim presented to General Amherst by John Mercer, August 1, 1759, in a letter carried to New York by George Mercer.[82]

Colonel George Mercer, as he was thereafter called, does not re-appear in public notice, nor in private correspondence, until January 1762, when he was again in Virginia at Williamsburg in the session of the Assembly as a burgess from Frederick County.[83] On the adjournment of the Assembly, he departed, carrying a letter of Governor Fauquier, of March 12, 1762, to Colonel Bouquet then in Pittsburgh.[84] On May 17, 1762, from Winchester, Colonel Mercer wrote Bouquet, "The Governor delivered me the Letter for you some Time-since, and I should have dispatched it immediately, but I believe it is now almost a month since I left Williamsburg." [85] His excuse was that he had been ill with ague and fever (malaria). He also said he was again just setting off for Philadelphia and expected to be there six weeks. And that is what he did. Writing to Colonel Bouquet, May 28, 1762, James Livingston said, "Colo Mercer is gone to Philada for Cloathing for the Regiment, with Orders for 6 s / Sterlg pr. yard for the private men." [86] He seems to have been back in military life. And Colonel Mercer himself says he was not present at the meeting of the Potomac Company in Frederick, Maryland, in May 1762 though he was "one of the two treasurers appointed, the other one being a Marylander," [87] and was greatly interested in the navigation of the Potomac.[88]

Domesticity Rejected

Bachelorhood as against matrimony was a matter of discussion in three or more letters of George Mercer to Henry Bouquet. Mercer did not praise the role of a bachelor except in relation to marriage as the alternative, one which he considered a gamble, particularly in the matter of congeniality. In two letters he uses the ambiguous word "Rambling" as descriptive of his bachelorhood. The first letter was written May 17, 1762, where he speaks of "roving and rambling

36

through the world for these eight Months past." [89]

On June 12, 1762, from Philadelphia, he wrote a long letter to Bouquet, then at Pittsburgh. Apology was made for neglect in not writing for some time and he acknowledged the justification of a scolding which Bouquet had indulged in. Matrimony is discussed at length and with a frankness which, as Mercer said, could be exercised only between confident friends. One sentence says, "I am greatly pleased to find my Resolution of quitting the military life approved of by so good a Judge, and more especially as I think it the first necessary step towards what you so strongly recommend on another occasion leaving off rambling and becoming a Man of serious Character, if any thing could effect such a change." [90] No comment on this is called for, but it can be seen that Bouquet was a wise man as well as a good friend and that George Mercer had self-acknowledged shortcomings and weaknesses, which in turn may have been responsible for some of the frustrations of his life.

From Philadelphia in late June, Colonel Mercer went to New York to settle more Virginia accounts with General Amherst. On his return to Philadelphia he wrote Bouquet, August 12, 1762.[91] "I went to New York," he said. "I made a five weeks Trip of it and am now just returned." For the third time he launched into a discussion of women and of married life. He must have seen many unhappy marriages and families. Like George Bernard Shaw two centuries later, he looked upon matrimony as an "irrational knot." "I have," he wrote, "seen so many Devils after the Ceremony." But he thought also of other matters such as his "Plantation in Virginia on Shenandoah River" where grass was abundant and where, after the manner of his father, he was engaged in the breeding of pure blood horses. An invitation was extended to Bouquet who had a large estate in nearby Maryland, to send his mares to Mercer's plantation for breeding with his blooded stallions.

In regard to Philadelphia, Bouquet said "The News of the Place" was "so trifling" as to be unworthy of mention. "One half of it," he wrote, "is scandal and the rest Family Affairs." He announced, "I set out this very day for Virginia." [92]

Information about Colonel Mercer in late August and throughout September 1762 has not been found. In early October he was at "Ourry Park," probably a place in the Allegheny Mountains, near Fort Bedford. A surviving fragment of his letter of October 6, 1762, from "Ourry Park" mentions the King's horses, lost, strayed or stolen but recoverable. Many of them, he thought, were in Frederick County,

Virginia, and, in his opinion, could be recovered by offering rewards for their recovery.[93]

A deed to Benjamin Hart for 973 acres at the price of £ 200, made in Loudoun County, November 7, 1762, by John Hough as attorney-in-fact for John Mercer . . . George Mercer . . . and James Mercer concerns George Mercer, in that he probably got £ 50 as his half of a moiety of "All that Tract" on Limestone Run.

Political and Social Interlude

In November 1762 George Mercer was at the Assembly in Williamsburg as a burgess from Frederick County. His brother James Mercer who owned two properties at Bath (later Berkeley Springs) was present as a burgess from recently established Hampshire County.[94]

While in Williamsburg, George Mercer presented a personal petition (not found) "praying that he may be allowed some satisfaction for the Trouble he was at, and the Expenses he incurred, in attending the Commissioners appointed by his Excellency Sir Jeffry Amherst at New York for settling the Accounts of the Expenses of this Colony for the Campaign of the year 1760." [95] It was "Resolved, That the Petition . . . is reasonable and that he ought to be allowed the Sum of £ 500 for his Services." The Council agreed[96] and the Governor signed the act December 23, 1762.[97] This was highly generous treatment. Here again Mercer was successful and not frustrated. He now had a nice sum of available money. There were many possible uses for it.

What followed is best stated by Mercer in a letter of January 9, 1763, to his friend, Colonel Bouquet. "Your Favour of 26th October was near two months Travelling to me at Williamsburg and our Session of Assembly was as tedius; at last We go a Holy Day on the 24th Decr. just time enough for me to ride to Westover to take my Christmas Dinner. Here I have remained ever since." [98] He was now a guest of his old Second Virginia Regiment Colonel, William Byrd III. It was a lively social experience. Among the other guests at Westover was the sister of Mrs. William Byrd, Anne Willing of Philadelphia, the object of devotion of Colonel Bouquet. This item alone indicates that Colonel Mercer when in Philadelphia enjoyed association with the cream of its social circles. In this letter, Mercer said, "I expect to be home in a Fortnight" and that he would be in Fredericksburg in Virginia, which he claimed as the place of his "abode." [99]

38

But on January 30, 1763, he was still a guest at Westover as is seen in his letter of that date to Colonel Bouquet, a letter in which he comments upon the Westover Christmas party and makes a notable statement about Virginia friendliness and hospitality, really about life in planter circles with which he was highly familiar. But "In Virginia Sir," he added, "We have Christmas always, at least there is generally good Cheer a hearty Welcome and indifferent Company to be met with." [100]

Reversion to Ohio Company Activities

Presumably George Mercer in early February 1763 was in Fredericksburg and probably at times at Marlborough and at Gunston Hall in conferences with James Mercer, John Mercer, George Mason and other regional members of the Ohio Company. He was not yet clear of contracts connected with past military campaigns,[101] but he was most concerned with the possibility of promoting the welfare of the Ohio Company around Wills Creek, Maryland, and across the Potomac in Virginia. The leaders of the Ohio Company, probably after a discussion with George Mercer about the situation on the Monongahela and on the Upper Potomac, decided to realize something from their property near Wills Creek. By the Articles of Agreement of May 23, 1751,[102] the Committee of the Ohio Company had executive power to act. A notice, unusually elaborate, of a meeting of the Ohio Company was drawn up and submitted to the newspapers for publication. It appeared in the *Maryland Gazette*, Annapolis, Maryland, February 17, 1763, and in the *Pennsylvania Gazette,* February 24, 1763, exactly one week later, all "By Order of the Committee of the Ohio Company." The meeting was called for "Tuesday the First of March . . . "

Not so clearly explicable, there appeared in the newspapers, with the above notice a lengthy advertisement of the Sale of Ohio Company "Lots for a Town at Fort Cumberland" and for the sale of the New Store land and buildings just across the Potomac from the mouth of Wills Creek. The sale was advertised to take place on Friday, April 15, 1763. And this advertisement is signed by George Mercer, not by the Committee of the Ohio Company. The details in the advertisement belong in the history of the Ohio Company rather than in the biography of George Mercer.

What was proposed in early February was approved in an official "Meeting of a Committee of the Ohio Company at Stafford Court house on Wednesday the 2d day of March 1763." [103] George Mercer was probably present on this occasion. The end of the resolution to sell the Lots states, " . . . George Mason is hereby impowered and required to execute Deeds and Leases as above mentioned to the persons purchasing and taking up the said Lotts or that he make a power of Attorney into Colo. George Mercer to execute and acknowledge the said Deeds and Leases in his name and that John Mercer Esq. be requested to draw up a Form for the said Deeds and Leases and power of Attorney according to the above mentioned Terms."

In a Real Estate Subdivision Scheme, 1763

It is probable that George Mercer hurried to Wills Creek to survey or lay out the lots as mentioned in the advertisement of February 17, 1763, and now enjoined in the resolution of March 2, 1763. It is virtually certain that he did not remain near Marlborough and Gunston Hall until John Mercer had drawn up the Form for the said Deeds and Leases and Power of Attorney and George Mason had signed the Power of Attorney, which was signed and recorded in the last week of March. It is reasonable to suppose that he left for Wills Creek, or Fort Cumberland about March 5, 1763, and reached his destination early in the second week of the month; that he made shortly his rough survey notes known as the Field Notes for the Charlottesburg Survey and made preparations for the sale announced for April 15, 1763. He bade fair to become the founder of Cumberland, Maryland, a quarter of a century before this role fell to Thomas Beall, son of Samuel. But another frustration of his career arose. Though largely in ruins and almost abandoned, Fort Cumberland was of military importance in case of a violent Indian uprising, of which vague rumors were circulating among Indian traders and at distant military posts. Rumors that the military authorities would probably re-occupy the area and seize any houses found there stopped the prospects of any sale on April 15, 1763. As George Mercer expressed it in the printed *Case*, p. 29, "the company . . . *sent* one of their members *from Virginia, to the commander in chief of the kings* forces at New York, on purpose to obtain his leave *to build a town on their own lands.*" [104] There is little, if any, doubt that the emissary was George Mercer. The fact that he did not name himself as such can be attributed to the modesty required in such a document. The fact that he underlined the statement may well indicate that it was a personal revelation which greatly affected him. It is worth notice, that if this be correct, George Mercer claims to have been, in 1763, a member of the Ohio Company, possibly as a result of his father's deed of November 1759.

From Fort Cumberland to Philadelphia was more than two hundred miles. If George Mercer returned to the lower Potomac for discussion and instructions, the distance was more nearly two hundred and fifty miles. It was a week's trip by horseback. On or before March 28, 1763, he was in Philadelphia, for a letter of Bouquet to Amherst March 28, 1763 is endorsed "To Sir Jeffery Amherst, 27th March 1763 by Coll. Geo. Mercer." [105] Probably a conference with Bouquet in Philadelphia was a matter of a day or two. Mercer, therefore, must have left Fort Cumberland not later than March 18, 1763, after a stay there of about two weeks. From Philadelphia, Mercer went on to New York which he reached on or before March 31, 1763. On March 31, 1763, Captain Gavin Cochrane, writing from New York, to Colonel Bouquet, remarked, "I happened to be with Coll. Robertson when I had the pleasure of yours by Colonel Mercer, and showed it to him," [106] and General Amherst, writing to Colonel Bouquet April 3, 1763, from New York, said, "Colonel Mercer Arrived here a few days ago, and Delivered me Your Letter of the 27th March." [107] In the printed *Case* of 1770, George Mercer described the interview with Amherst, who refused his assent to the subdivision of the lands. This refusal of Amherst was an injury to the interests of the Ohio Company and another frustration of the career of George Mercer who, if not so unfortunately rebuffed in this project, might have spent many profitable years, financial and otherwise, in real estate operations along Wills Creek and the upper Potomac.

According to his own account,[108] George Mercer returned to Fort Cumberland and on April 15, 1763, met the would-be purchasers of lots, reported the decision of General Amherst and its acceptance, for the time being, by the Ohio Company and called off the sale while forbidding any occupation or settlement of the Company's land.

In the meantime, while Colonel Mercer was in Philadelphia, George Mason signed the Power of Attorney to George Mercer, and had it recorded at Frederick County Courthouse, Frederick, Maryland, March 29, 1763.[109] Probably written by John Mercer, though the original in his inimitable handwriting has not been found, the document on record reiterates ideas and plans already advertised February 17, 1763, and outlined in the Ohio Company resolution of March 2, 1763. Since the power of attorney assigned to George Mercer was abortive, it has the historical value only of a factuality and of a testimony to confidence at the time in the ability and integrity of Mercer. It may therefore be merely mentioned.

Colonel Mercer evidently left Fort Cumberland in April. He

probably stopped for a few days at Winchester and at his plantation on the Shenandoah in the morning shadow of the Blue Ridge. In May he was in Williamsburg as one of the Burgesses from Frederick County.[110] While he was in Williamsburg, Abraham Traxell, a Pennsylvania German and probably a tenant on Bouquet's Maryland lands, wrote Bouquet, June 13, 1763, from "Long Meadow" that he had sent the best mares to Colonel Mercer's place where they would be permitted to remain until ready and fit for work.[111]

On June 16, 1763, there was published in the *Maryland Gazette* another notice of a Meeting of the Ohio Company, this one to be held at Stafford Courthouse on Monday, July 4, 1763. Somewhat remarkably, under the circumstances, this newspaper issue of June 16, 1763, contains another long, somewhat revised, advertisement of the sale of the Ohio Company property on Wills Creek and at the New Store settlement, a matter so abortive as to receive little or no attention in the records of the time. In fact, as eventualities were to reveal, the Ohio Company had decided upon a different policy. It would appeal again as of old to the authorities in London, to the King in Council.

Projected Appeal to the Crown

As early as 1759, George Mercer had considered a trip to Europe,[112] though his motivation is nowhere revealed. He may have been thinking of military bounties promised by Governor Dinwiddie. He may have hoped to secure confirmation to the Ohio Company of the old lands of the Company along the lower Monongahela, now cleared of the enemy in late 1759. He may have hoped for preferment as an imperial colonial official and he may have wished to travel abroad and see the old world as so many of his fellow colonial aristocrats were in the habit of doing. After his rebuff by Amherst in April 1763 and the frustration of his real estate plans along the upper Potomac, he determined, it seems, to go to Europe. His plans antedate the meeting of the Ohio Company at Stafford Courthouse July 4, 1763. He evidently submitted a memorial to the Governor and Council of Virginia, for in Document B, Rockingham Papers[113] is found much biographical data best revealed in its original format of June 16, 1763:

Upon Consideration of a Memorial of George Mercer Esqr. produced and read this day in Council, setting forth that he has been long engaged in the Service and Defense of this Colony and is now determined upon going to Europe to sollicit his Majesty for some Employment, and requesting such Recommendation from this Board as they shall think him deserving of.

We the Lieutenant-Governor, and Council do, with the highest satisfaction and the most religious regard to Truth, hereby testify that the said

42

George Mercer has for many years served in the Troops of this Colony, was Lieutenant Colonel of a Regiment, and always beloved as a brave active and Gallant Officer — That he has often been employed by the Government in many important Services, and has ever discharged the Trusts reposed in him with the greatest Expedition, Exactness and Fidelity: That his Conduct in every Station and upon all occasions as well in a private as public capacity has been such we have observed with Pleasure and can commend with Justice.

A letter of the Committee of Correspondence of Virginia to Edward Montague, June 17, 1763, is of similar character and purport. It said, "Colo Mercer who will deliver you this, was one of those Officers, being at first appointed a Captain. But as he distinguished himself by his Gallant Behaviour, was promoted to the Rank of a Lieutenant Colonel, in which office he gained universal Applause. This Gent. goes home to endeavr. to be in some manner rewarded for his faithful services and you are desired to introduce him properly and influence in his Favr. Besides, this our Recommendation, we doubt not but his Conduct and Behavior will be such as to entitle him to your Favr. and Protection." [114]

However skeptical one may be about the validity and value, in general, of testimonials, it is, in the light of the independent origins of these statements, impossible to conceive of more favorable statements about anyone. Colonel George Mercer was, at the age of thirty, in good military, social and political standing in Virginia in the middle of June 1763. His several frustrations of the previous decade had not yet produced anything resembling total or complete external frustration.

With such public approval and with such preliminary activity on his own part, it was natural that George Mercer was selected and appointed as the member to represent the Ohio Company at London in the near future. At the meeting of July 4, 1763, there was introduced a petition to be presented to the King. Probably prepared earlier by John Mercer and approved by Philip Ludwell Lee and Thomas Ludwell Lee, members of the Committee, it was signed by them and four additional members of the Company. [115]

An interesting and somewhat personal document of the meeting was the holograph George Mercer item, saying, "The members present approve of the Terms recommended by their Committee at their last Meeting proposed by Colo. George Mercer to sollicit their Grant in England; and agree that their Treasurer do give Credit to Messrs. Hanbury's Account with the Company, for the Amount of Mr. Samuel Smith's Share of the Company's Lands and Stock and close Mr. Smith's Account in the Company's Books by Credit for the same." [116] The nine members present signed this document. But in addition to this item, it was "Resolved that the Company will upon the very first Notice from Colo Mercer reimburse and repay him any Sums of money which he shall judge necessary to expend in order to obtain a Grant for the Ohio Company on the terms they have now Petitioned for provided the Sum does not exceed two thousand pounds sterling in the whole, including any money that may be advanced or raised by Charlton Palmer Esqr. on this Accot." [117] Certainly an indication of confidence in his procedure, this resolution was, nevertheless, only a limited *carte blanche* in finances. Anything different financially would have been poor business. The confidence is well expressed in the text of the Ohio Company's Appointment and Instructions to George Mercer,[118] the first paragraph of which is: "Sir From our Knowledge of you, We trusting in your Skill, abilities and Address, do as members of the Ohio Company, impower you to sollicit for that Company according to the following Instructions."

The instructions were "to proceed as soon as convenient to London," to consult Dinwiddie and the Hanburys, to act jointly with Charlton Palmer in the presentation of the petition, to wait upon Lord Halifax asking his patronage, to write the Company frequently and to settle "the Company's Account with Messrs. Hanbury, and use few Words but say them often."

Several items in the Instructions require specific attention. One mentions the Petition "which you now have with you." Another mentions "our state Case which Mr. Palmer has." Yet another speaks of "the Papers you have with you" (possibly copies of official records).

The last paragraph sagely remarked, "We doubt not of your Oconomy in the Expences, and of your Dispatch in returning to Us . . . " On these points there may have been no doubt in the minds of fellow members and friends in 1763, but on the basis of eventualities these ideas were later to be far short of realization.

Evidently Colonel Mercer did not sail immediately for England, though he left Marlborough July 6, 1763.[119] Governor Fauquier wrote to the Board of Trade, July 8, 1763, in the letter referred to Mercer as an authority on Indian matters, and sent the letter to England by Mercer. The new London agent of the Ohio Company remarks in the *Case,* of 1770 (p. 31), "Their agent arrived in London in September 1763."

Thus came about a profound and critical change in the career of George Mercer. What he might have accomplished if he had remained in Virginia is a matter of interesting speculation. He might have later received military promotion such as came to Washington, Hugh Mercer, William Weedon, William W. Woodward, Henry Lee, Daniel Morgan and other friends and neighbors of Colonel George Mercer. He might have gone far in politics and become a governor as did his younger half-brother, John Francis Mercer. He might have grown in wealth and power with the expanding western frontier of Virginia and Kentucky. But he turned away from these possibilities and with exception of about three months in the autumn of 1765, spent the rest of his life in Europe.

PART II
Voluntary Exile, 1763—1784

Emotional Conflict

IN the years between 1750 and 1783 the old conflict of interests and idealogies within the so-called British Empire became in one generation so acute as to produce fission and warfare. There were naturally serious emotional conflicts in the case of individuals. The issue was imperialism versus regionalism or what soon became nationalism. Tradition, legalism, constitutionalism, interests, rights and other things became a matter of emotional conflict. There is, from somewhat scanty data, evidence of such conflict or conflicts in the case of George Mercer.

Hope Deferred, 1763-1765

In remarkably concise yet highly comprehensive statement, George Mercer said he, on his arrival in London, "immediately waited on the secretary of state with this memorial, which he told him he would inform his majesty of, and that he should be commanded to attend with it, whenever his majesty would be pleased to receive it; but no orders were ever sent him on the subject: and on the 7th of October following his majesty was pleased to issue his royal proclamation, forbidding any grants or settlements to the westward of the Allegheny mountains." [120] Thus here at the very beginning of his solicitation or agency in London, he ran headlong into a serious frustration, one which was more ominous than he could have anticipated. It would seem to many that the circumstances mentioned when added to the bad situation of John Mercer's finances, the losses and failures of the Ohio Company and the terms and words of his instructions should have led George Mercer to return to Virginia in October 1763. In his own words, "This proclamation being a total bar for the present to the company's design, their agent [George Mercer] hoping it was only intended to remedy some temporary inconveniences, which would of themselves be immediately removed, thought it advisable to wait that event, and therefore took no farther steps till the year 1765." [121] Written several years after 1763 this statement seems to be tinged with both sincere truth and neat apology.

Two Letters of Importance, 1763-1764

There have been located by the writer of this sketch, only two letters of George Mercer which were written in the first twelve months of his stay in Europe. One of these, to Captain Thomas Rutherford of Winchester, Virginia, was written October 28, 1763. While somewhat reasonably it says nothing about his role in Ohio Company business, it embraces some military matters, some regional items and gossipy information about himself, his work and London society and politics.[122]

A much more extended and confidential letter to his brother, March 11, 1764, has been found in the Kentucky Collection of the Western State College, Bowling Green, Kentucky, a letter which may have been left behind in Kentucky by Charles Fenton Mercer who once resided for some years at Carrollton, Kentucky. This rambling letter about himself and London politics and society furnishes the best information available on George Mercer in London in his first year of residence there. In it he mentions the "Great Difficulties I have met with already" and the "Delays the Ohio Company oblige me to make by not sending me the proper Papers." He pronounced that "Nothing shall engage me to take a Winter's Passage, they are both dangerous and disagreeable." His most descriptive statement about his agency was that "During the Session of Parliament the Great ones will meddle with Nothing but Parliamentary Matters: so soon as it rises, they go into the Country for a Recess, and in Summer 'tis known little Business is ever done, so that I think the month of October seems already pointed out to me as the soonest they'll think of my Affairs."

In this letter he also mentions "two Packets from My Father and you" but says, "I have not received a Letter from a man in Virginia out of our Family, my Father and yourself meaning, except from Mr. Yates recommending me to his Mother . . ."

Among more personal matters Colonel Mercer said he was negotiating for a brewer for his father, that he had shipped a "Groce of Bottles, two pair of large millstones, iron work and Boulting Cloths" for his mill in Frederick County, a pair of small millstones for the mill on Little River, and two fine young rams, one for his own plantation and the other to be kept at Marlborough. London he claimed to dislike, saying, ". . . London — the Lord send me safe out of it I say."

London merchants he pronounced the "most conceited, upstart, impertinent Fellows I ever saw." With Samuel Athawes he got into a quarrel about Virginia financial legislation, calling him a liar for denouncing the legislators as thieves. At this date, Mercer could say, "Messrs. Hanbury . . ." have been "tolerably civil to me." Athawes was sharply criticized for delaying many weeks packets sent George Mercer by John Mercer in October 1763 and James Mercer in November 1763. Future mail he wanted sent to Wm. Hunter of London.

The life of George Mercer in London is at least partly revealed. He follows another statement, ". . . upon my Honour no poor Wretch was ever tired of Captivity more than I am of London," with the additional data, ". . . I have been obliged to attend here all this Time, without pleasing or even amusing myself, or doing any one else any Kind of Service I sit at Home and read all Day, at Night I shut the Book and go to Bed, as I own twice is as much as ever I choose to see a play and some have pleased a Number, and been continued for 40 or 50 Nights together."

As a mercantile center, Colonel Mercer preferred Bristol to London. As a place of residence he preferred Bath. "I passed my Time tolerably at Bath where I continued upwards of two months, but here it hangs heavy on my Hands." About London he wrote, ". . . I believe too it is the dearest place in the whole World: I can not even sit at Home under a Guinea a Day, and if you go and keep Company 5 or 6 [guineas] sometimes are melted." Enclosing a bill for a dinner, he stated it cost three friends 16 guineas, his share of which he escaped by being indisposed and absent.

After a brief discussion of tobacco shipments and prices Colonel Mercer took up the matter of old military accounts. He sharply condemns Colonel Lewis (presumably Fielding Lewis) for protesting George Mercer's order in favor of Dr. Sutherland, saying of Lewis, he "must have imbibed from Contact some W—sh— Principles." Mercer claimed he had been forced to meet payments from "the very money too for which I gave Dr. Walker my bond and you know I pay interest for."

A long paragraph deals with the relations of Colonel Mercer and George Washington. The pronouns are so indefinite as to produce uncertainty. Mercer claimed he had trouble about settlements for a period of eight years. The last sentence is both striking and revealing. "The Services I was of to Col. Washington the Country in some measure rewarded me for — though he might have afforded to have done it himself out of his Allowance and the Reputation he obtained by it — but thank God, I have done with him, and if he will pay off the Account, I am sure I never desire to deal with him again." In this matter one may find a partial explanation of George Mercer's failure to return to America on the outbreak of war in 1775.

48

In the latter half of the letter, he mentions his mills, saying, "I expect they will clear me a good Income when they are finished." He claims to have initiated legislation in England providing bounties of importance for hemp; and to have pressed the Board of Trade for the free importation from Portugal of salt for colonial cattle.

A short paragraph says, "As I hope and expect so much to be at Home this Fall, . . . Let me beg you in the mean Time to make me all the Remittances my Estate will afford, as there is no breathing here, scarce without Money," a significant request in that the writer at this date, in early 1764, says nothing about claims on members of the Ohio Company.

Referring probably to lands in Fairfax County, tracts held in common by George and James Mercer, he wrote, "I am glad Carlyle and you did not conclude the Bargain about the Land as it certainly must be worth more than £ 415 — but whatever you do I shall approve of in every particular."

Domestic matters are found in a short paragraph in which he first felicitates James Mercer on his marriage, saying, "I give you Joy on commencing Housekeeper, and hope you may always be as well pleased with it, as you appear to be at present," then says, "I am much obliged to you for your kind offer, and think it is probable, I may billet myself upon you when I come over," a statement indicating that George Mercer had no residence of his own, in Fredericksburg.

The third item is on the familiar theme of marriage, saying, ". . . I have not the least Suspicion of importing a Female with me, as I have conceived a greater Aversion if possible than ever to Matrimony since I came to England." A long paragraph deals with American colonial boys sent to school in England but there neglected alike by the merchants who placed them and by the schools in which they were placed.

Some attention is then given to some personal property left behind in Virginia, some of it "Leather Stocks" and "Bottles of perfume, jars of raisins and almonds, boxes of candles and 100 lb. of Chocolate." More important, "Also were left there, I mean at Colo Lewis' house my property a Mahogany Desk and Book Case, and a Set of Steel Springs for a Chariot, these last Articles (the Steel Springs) I desire may be sent me here," this last an interesting request in the light of his proposed early return to Virginia.

London weather, a perennial topic of travellers, is roundly condemned in the statement, "I intend over to Ireland as soon as the Weather is settled, if ever it will, to see my Aunts. There never was such a Season known to me I assure you — on my Honor the Sun has not shone two Days together since I have been in England and it rained above two months without a single hour of clear Weather the Whole Time."

"With Compliments and greetings to all Friends" he wanted them assured that he was well.

Activities, 1764-1765

Of George Mercer's activities and life from March 1764 to April 1765 little is definitely revealed by documents available. He had written that he was going to Ireland and he may have gone there in 1764 and spent the winter there. In his several memorials of later years he claimed he was in Ireland when the Stamp Act was under consideration by the ministry and parliament. But that he had returned to London before April 4, 1765, is revealed in his letter of that date to Benjamin Franklin about answers to queries sent from the Stamp Office to him and to Franklin, and asking permission to peruse Franklin's answers to the queries and somewhat strangely pleading his own incapability and professing his ignorance about answers to the queries. At the time Mercer's address was Poland Street No. 9.[123] In a later memorial Colonel Mercer claimed he was in London, acting in connection with the production of stamps, from April 6 to September 1765.

Ohio Company Business

But meanwhile, he was not unmindful of his position as agent of the Ohio Company, and contemporary with his attention to stamps, he was alert about his regular responsibility. As he himself stated the matter, ". . . being informed that several families in Virginia within the limits described by that proclamation [of October 7, 1763], who had been in actual possession, obtained grants, paid quit rents, and every demand of government for several years, had petitioned the general assembly to represent their case to his majesty, as being under that proclamation, deprived of their property, he judged it proper to present the following humble memorial, as well as that which the company had sent over with him in 1763 to his majesty." [124] Though based, possibly, on documents in his possession, this memorial of George Mercer of June 21, 1765, was his own work buttressed as it was by his own knowledge and experience.

In the first paragraph the memorialist introduced the imperial problem of possession of the interior of North America and relations with the Indians. As printed in the *Case*, of 1770, (pp. 32-33), the

50

paragraphs carry marginal annotations. Among these are found the following: "Ohio Company raise a stock"; "Apply to the king for a grant of land"; "Bounds within which the company pray to take land"; "To settle 100 families in seven years, and erect a fort"; "Lord's report, Feb. 23, 1748-9"; "16 March, 1748-9"; [Instruction to grant], "above 10,000 [spent]"; "Obstructions from the French forces"; "1,350,000 acres granted" [to rival companies]; "Fort begun by the company, destroyed by the French," etc.

In a later paragraph he mentioned his mission and the acceptance of any royal decision. Then in a final petition he "Prays that instructions to the governor may be renewed or that it may be recommended to parliament to reimburse them their expenses or that lands may be given them in some other part of America."

This memorial of George Mercer, though based on the Company Memorial of July 4, 1763, and possibly influenced by Charlton Palmer and others, shows that George Mercer was willing to do something more than merely hand in papers of others and solicit their reception and fulfilment.

Another frustration was in store for Colonel Mercer. As he put it, "These memorials his majesty in council, 21st of June, 1765, was graciously pleased to refer to the right honourable the Lords for trade and plantations, with directions to report what might be advisable to be done thereupon; and their lordships, for reasons assigned, did not take up the consideration of them till the year 1767 . . ." [125] This of course meant four years of frustrating delay and four years of equally troublesome expenses, little or none of which were met by the Ohio Company but fell mainly upon George Mercer.

After two years in London, George Mercer should have realized that the frustrations of Fort Necessity, 1754, Braddock's campaign, 1755, and the subdivision of lands of 1763 were simple and clear, compared with the intricacies and whirlpools of British politics. But such was seemingly not the case. In 1765 he became involved in the most notorious and probably the dominant frustration of his life and career.

Stamp Act Involvement, 1765

In 1764 a new British imperial policy was put forward. The customs service was reinvigorated, new revenue acts were passed and a stamp act was projected, but delayed in enactment for about twelve months. Then on March 22, 1765, the famous Stamp Act was approved by Parliament and assented to by the King. News of the passing of the Act reached America in a few weeks. With the opposition to the Stamp Act all students of American history are familiar. But with the course of events in London they are less so. George Grenville doggedly went ahead with the program, which to him and most residents of England seemed reasonable. But as a conciliatory matter, he proposed to appoint colonials as stamp distributors and asked the colonial agents at London to nominate candidates. It has long been known, or at least suspected, that the Franklins of Philadelphia and the Lees of Stratford Hall were trapped by such enticement. More direct information is that of Jared Ingersoll of Connecticut. In a newspaper item of September 1765, he reported, "There happened but three instances of persons then on the spot belonging to the old Continent Colonies to whom ye offer was made, who were in a Condition to accept it personally. These were Colo Mercer from Virginia and Mr. Massarve, Son of ye late Coll Massarve from New Hampshire, who happened accidentally in London at that time on business of their own and myself." [126] The names of the stamp distributors were announced in London in early August. George Mercer, in a memorial of April 11, 1766, said, "my Commission was made out on the 2d of August." [127] He may have been, as he said later in Williamsburg, absent from London on a trip to Ireland at the time of the passage of the Act, but he did accept the position of stamp distributor and, by his own statement a decade later, was promised it as early as April 6, 1765. No explanation by him of his reasons is very specific. He probably thought the Act was constitutional and the position of stamp distributor one of honorable governmental service. Probably he thought this service to the Ministry and the King might result in more favorable consideration of the interests and rights of the Ohio Company. And he was in need of money and personal income, a matter mentioned by his father in 1768.[128] Probably if it had not been for his financial distress he might have escaped this trap and much of the later frustration of his life. From his portrait and from remarks of his friends, one may suspect that George Mercer was somewhat naive.

George Mercer sailed from England, September 12, 1765, on board the *Leeds,* bringing with him stamps for Virginia and also for Maryland and North Carolina.[129] He arrived in Virginia October 29, 1765, and reached Williamsburg the following evening. He probably did not fully realize that the Stamp Act had aroused a fury which had spread throughout the colony, since Patrick Henry's resolutions of late May. The events of the next twenty-four hours were the dramatic crisis of his life. The old army officer was not intimidated by the crowd which came to his quarters asking him to resign. He promised to consider the problem and make a later reply. He recognized the crowd as representative of the society of the region and the time. His situation, however, was probably more unfortunate than critical.

As revealed in contemporary accounts, notably in the newspapers of Virginia, Maryland and Pennsylvania, his behavior under the circumstances was not unworthy. And the behavior of Govenor Francis Fauquier was equally worthy and highly honorable. The governor's position was in the balance. He joined Colonel Mercer in facing the crowd. His duty was to promote the enforcement of the Act as well as to maintain order and peace. But Colonel Mercer, while maintaining the rectitude of his position and behavior, recognized the strength of popular opposition and in a declaration or address to the crowd, in a genteel manner declined "to act in an office so odious to his country." [130]

In the confusion and uproar, several discrepancies of statement and fact are recorded. In his memorial of April 11, 1766, Mercer stated, "I embarked seven Days from my Arrival in America." [131] But elsewhere he says he sailed on November 28, 1765, a full month after his arrival. He may have meant that he left Williamsburg probably by boat, for Annapolis and a northern seaport. Governor Fauquier had Colonel Mercer before himself in Council and, in a Certificate, said Colonel Mercer "declared before me in Council that he did not bring with him, or was ever charged by the Commissioners of Customs in England with the care of any Stamps," [132] while all the time the stamps were on shipboard off the shore. Colonel Mercer himself later said his action was motivated by a desire to conceal the location of the stamps and thus prevent their destruction. By the action of both Colonel Mercer and Governor Fauquier the stamps were removed from the *Leeds* and "lodged . . . for Safety, with Captain Stirling on board the *Rainbow.*" Mercer in his letter of November 10, 1765, to Governor Horatio Sharpe of Maryland stated flatly, "I had the Stamps for three Provinces in Charge, and dared not let any one know where they were." Here one finds necessity as the mother of deception, possibly justifiable deception. The cherry tree story comes to one's mind.

From Williamsburg, George Mercer, eleven (not seven) days after his arrival, wrote November 10, 1765, to Governor Horatio Sharpe of Maryland.[133] He mentions having seen Philip Sharpe, the Governor's brother, just before leaving London for Williamsburg;

he discussed his trouble in Williamsburg; comments on the stamps on board the ship and intended for Maryland, and says, "I find myself under a Necessity of returning immediately to England." Yet George Mercer issued a Power of Attorney to his brother James Mercer to act in his behalf in regard to the safety and distribution of the stamps on board the *Rainbow* and endorsed it "Given at Williamsburgh, under my Hand and Seal, this 18th day of November 1765." [134] According to his memorial of April 11, 1766, George Mercer left Virginia on November 28, 1765, four full weeks after his arrival. He did not go to Marlborough to visit with his father, who in 1768 wrote his son George, "But your Letter which, to my great surprise, informed me of your intentions of going to England, before I had an opportunity of one days conversation with you . . ." Posterity may well be equally surprised. The issue was settled the last of October. One wonders why in four full weeks he could not make a short trip to visit his old friends and his relatives. The reasons were probably psychic and emotional rather than a matter of filial impiety. Actually he had seen his father in Williamsburg on his arrival late in October. Yet another problem of his biography is why he returned to England.

By declining to carry on his work as distributor of stamps, he had regained the good will of the populace. His military career was unsullied. He held possession of several large tracts of land and additional pieces of real estate. By the gubernatorial proclamation of 1754 and the Royal Proclamation of October 7, 1763, he was entitled to many thousands of acres of military bounty land. He had remained a burgess for Frederick County even when staying abroad. Seemingly he had much to gain by remaining in Virginia. But his decision was otherwise. Prospects of a "Winter's Passage . . . both dangerous and disagreeable" did not, on this occasion, deter him. Sailing on November 28, 1765, he arrived in England at the end of the third week in January and appeared before a Committee of the House of Commons January 31, 1766, and February 12, 1766. An interesting historical statistic is found in his testimony that "The Scheme I had formed for distribution would have required 25 Distributors." Ten years later he put in an expense account for three clerks employed for a three year period. He must have projected more than a score of American assistant distributors.

"Why did you leave Virginia?" was a question asked him by the Committee. His answer was: "Findg. an opposition — The Govr. wod. not let me Resign and the people wod. not let me Execute it. I thot. it my Duty to return to inform the psons appointing me." [135]

John Mercer, in January 1768, wrote his son, "I fully approved of your Resolution and Reasons" for going back to England. It is not difficult to sympathize with this sense of honor and duty. Like the soldier that he was, he had to make his report and render his account, however unfavorable it would seem to those whom he served. And there are indications that friends had bonded him for the stamps and he wished to save losses to them by explaining to the government what had happened. It is reasonable also to conjecture that his 1763 hopes of imperial employment and preferment may not have died out at this time.

To one familiar with the history of the Ohio Company as recently revealed by additional materials, it is obvious that he still hoped to get lands or recompense for the Company. The two memorials handed in June 21, 1765, were still before the Board of Trade and Plantations. No one could know what might happen, that yet another year would pass before any action would be taken. His future was a gamble. In a sense he hung between two worlds, the world of the British Empire and the, as yet merely imaginative, world of nascent American nationalism. It would seem that he acted unwisely, that he gambled and lost. But politically his motives may have been beyond ethical reproach.

John Mercer, writing in January 1768, about the letter to him by George Mercer, November 1765, said it "assured me that you would not stay in England an hour longer than was necessary to justify your own conduct and Indemnify your Securities." [136] This understanding was in vain. The available records indicate that George Mercer never again returned to America.

Ohio Company Affairs, 1766-1770

For three or more years, George Mercer in London was busy with Ohio Company matters. He seems also to have been emotionally involved with English women, one of whom he married in 1767 as will be mentioned later. He doubtless had a stable, for he "fell off" his horse,[137] though fortunately without "ill consequences." And he probably felt himself, as he actually was in America, discredited by the stamp distribution episode. Regardless of his financial trouble, London with its faint hope of political preferment may have seemed to him better than a life of unpopularity in Virginia.

Probably George Mercer wrote to his brother James Mercer in February 1766, as indicated in an item in the *Virginia Gazette,* April 11, 1766, announcing a letter from George Mercer in the post office. He also wrote to his father March 27, 1766.[138] On April 11, 1766,

55

after the repeal of the Stamp Act, he put in an application to the Marquis of Rockingham whose government had ended an episode by the repeal. "The Memorial which Mercer submitted is now in the City Library at Sheffield, England, among the letters and papers of this same Marquis of Rockingham." [139] A long document, it involves the customary introduction, a statement that Mercer was in military service until the Proclamation of Peace in 1763, that he was made a Colonel in July 1761, that he settled the Virginia accounts with Stanwix and the Cherokee accounts with Amherst, that Grenville in 1765 appointed him "Chief Distributor of the Stamps in Virginia" and he was commissioned on August 6, 1765. His request for recompense for his trouble and service was just, but its consideration was delayed and never carried through. The Rockingham ministry was quickly displaced. In June 1766 Colonel Mercer put in a similar memorial, now found in the Dartmouth Manuscripts, Volume II.[140]

Bearing not upon the life of George Mercer in 1766 but upon his career in 1765 in connection with stamp trouble, there appeared in the *Virginia Gazette* in the summer and autumn of 1766, a violent controversy between the Mercers and the Lees. Richard Henry Lee had led the criticism of George Mercer in October 1765 and George Mercer's father and brother James took up the cudgels in his defense. Writing on July 18, 1766, James Mercer claimed Richard Henry Lee had tried through friends to secure an appointment as stamp distributor but failed to get it and then turned to opposition and headed an attack on George Mercer. A few facts are revealed in the bitter items printed in the newspapers. He claimed that George Mercer went to Ireland in the fall of 1764, intending to return to Virginia in a spring passage, that friends secured the position for him during his absence and that he returned to London three months later. The burning of his effigy in Westmoreland County was condemned. It was alleged that in September or October 1765, Richard Henry Lee published his defense, or "Confession," in a Maryland newspaper. The implication is that Lee sheltered himself behind a vicious attack on George Mercer. On July 25, a short item, seemingly by John Mercer, continued the attack on Lee. A signed item of great length by John Mercer, September 26, 1766, furnishes some historical data of uncertain reliability. It says George Mercer entered military service in 1754 under Colonel Fry, that he stayed in military service until the peace treaty of 1763, that he spent £ 500 of his own money during the decade of military service, that the Virginia agent in London was responsible for his appointment as stamp distributor, that he arrived at

Hampton on October 29, 1765 and reached Williamsburg at 5:00 P.M. the following day. There is a vague implication that rather than either law or military service, George Mercer may well have gone into the use of "the plumb line and the square" and become a "Carpenter," so-called (now called architect) and possibly a surveyor.

A long letter of James Mercer, October 3, 1776, gives the text of George Mercer's declaration on his abdication of his position as distributor of stamps, October 31, 1765.

An anonymous item, from Fredericksburg, Virginia, October 10, 1766, contains bitter reproaches upon John Mercer and James Mercer for their newspaper writing. A newspaper item of March 28, 1786, says George Mercer reached London January 25, 1766.

On the very day of the appearance of the defense of George Mercer in the *Virginia Gazette,* George Mercer in London wrote, September 26, 1766, to his father. This letter like numerous others written by him has not survived, but it is mentioned by his father in January 1768.[141] The same is true of a similar letter of December 11, 1766. As John Mercer wrote, nearly a year later, one of the letters "came very opportunely to prevent the sale of the Shenandoah land and pursuant to your desire I and my wife and your brother executed a conveyance to you of the whole tract, which together with my wife's privy examination and acknowledgement of it was recorded the last general court, the deed bearing date the first of June to precede your marriage." The regard of his father, his brother and his step-mother for George Mercer certainly had not dimmed, for they were all financially embarrassed at that time.

George Mercer in June 1767 again put forward the claims of the Ohio Company. He evidently went first to John Pownall, the secretary of the Board of Trade. As its *Journal,* under date June 11, 1767, states (p. 395), "The Secretary acquainted the Board that he was desired by Colonel Mercer, of Virginia, to move their lordships to take into consideration a petition to his Majesty, in behalf of the Ohio Company, praying either that directions may be given to the Governor of that colony to carry their plan of settlement into execution, or that they may be reimbursed the Expenses they have been at which petition was reported to this Board on the 21st of June 1765, but no person appearing to prosecute the same, was not proceeded with." Under date June 18, 1767, the *Journal* (p. 397) mentions the "Report to the Lords of the Committee of Council upon the petition of Colonel Mercer, in behalf of the Ohio Company." But although ready on June 18th, the report was not submitted until June 26, 1767, and is com-

monly given that date. George Mercer was obviously in London in
the summer of 1767, dancing attendance upon imperial authorities.
He also found time, July 8, 1767, to write another letter to his
father.[142] Unfortunately this and other similar letters have not been
found and probably have not survived.

Personal Affairs

In these lost letters of George Mercer to his father, John Mercer,
and to his brother, James Mercer, hints of romances, courtships and
marriage must have been given by George Mercer. Rumor had it
that the young lady, the fiancée, was "Miss Smith of Scarborough," [143]
but as the *Gentleman's Magazine*, XXXVIL (August 1767, p. 429),
had it, under "List of Marriages for 1767," "Colonel Mercer of
North America to Miss Neville of Lincoln." One commentator has
stated, "George Mercer married on August 18, 1767 at Scarboro
England, Mary Neville, daughter of Christopher Neville [Nevell] of
Lincoln, who died without issue, in Richmond, Virginia, June 4, 1768.
It is said to have been a runaway match." [144] Another writer says,
"he revisited his native land, bringing with him an English bride.
This lady died in Richmond the following year and Colonel Mercer
soon after returned to London." [145] As will be shortly revealed, much
of this is inaccurate, high proof that neither relatives nor scholarly
research historians can be fully relied upon. It is as certain as any
historical fact that George Mercer was in London in 1767 and 1768.
It is unreasonable but not impossible that his new and perhaps young
wife may have come to America to meet her husband's relatives and
look into her husband's financial situation and that on a visit to
Richmond, possibly to be with or near William Byrd III, she may have
died there. Highly specialized research would be required to prove or
disprove this. The fact that such a visit by Mary Neville Mercer was
not indicated in his ledgers by John Mercer, nor commented upon in
his letters, seems to disprove the fact. If so, it was a romantic
tragedy, for most certainly her husband was not with her. For her,
death and burial would then have been on soil, distant and almost
foreign and strange.

As for Colonel Mercer, he wrote his father September 18,
1767;[146] he possibly had sheets printed about the *Case* of the Ohio
Company; he wrote and handed in to Lord Shelburne, October 8,
1767, a well organized and well stated document on the "Company's
Affairs";[147] he wrote, October 10, 1767, a long letter to the Committee of the Ohio Company;[148] wrote a letter to his father November

15, 1767;[149] wrote on November 21, 1767, to the Ohio Company;[150] wrote another letter to his father November 25, 1767;[151] and, late in November, put out and presented another memorial to the King in Council,[152] a document which was not taken up for consideration for two years and is therefore commonly dated as of November 20, 1769. No one in those days could have crossed the Atlantic while engaged in such activities. The situation remained the same in 1768. John Mercer wrote George three (and probably more) letters in early 1768. The first letter, finished January 28, 1768, is endorsed by George Mercer (presumably in London), "Letter from my Father dated January 28th 1768 — Reced at Bristol April 20th 1768." [153] A second letter of March 3, 1768, is endorsed, "Letter from my Father dated March 3d 1768 reced. 4th June . . . ," [154] which probably means received at London the fourth of June 1768, the day his wife is supposed to have died in Virginia. The third letter of March 9, 1768, carries no such endorsement of date received but may well have been received more than a week later, probably in mid-June.[155]

Better evidence, if needed, that George Mercer was not in Virginia but in London in early 1768 is an item of May 31, 1768, in the *Journal of the Board of Trade and Plantations* (pp. 29-30) as follows:

Colonel Mercer attending likewise pursuant to Order, was heard upon the subject matter of the address of the House of Burgesses for leave to settle westward of the Alleghany Mountains and after stating to their lordships the improvements that had been made by the settlers under grants, prior to the Proclamation of October 1763 and the hardships they had suffered by being removed from their settlements, he withdrew.

Probably in August 1768, he wrote to Mr. Nickolson[156] and on August 16, 1768, he wrote a long letter, probably to James Mercer.[157] It begins with praise of Lord Botetourt as the incoming successor of Francis Fauquier, suggesting that he be well received and saying he has as "I know, one of the prettiest seats in England, as I have often visited it with great pleasure," subtle suggestion that Colonel Mercer in England associated with the gentry as well as with merchants and possibly with adventurers like himself.

He asked his brother to let it be known to the people of Virginia, "I have a promise that the accounts due them, since the campaign under Braddock, and all claims on the Crown shall be paid them," adding to this the statement, "Lord Botetourt can tell you the steps I have taken in that business." Definitely autobiographical data are furnished in his statement, "If you receive any money for me, it will not be disagreeable to me to have it remitted, as the difficulty of getting money here is inconceivable." This is buttressed by the remark, "If a gentleman merchant lends you, after begging, praying, beseeching, importuning, etc., etc., he is sure to tell it to all the trades, and though you tell him you cannot pay him under six months, he will be sure to ask you for it every week of the time." Not then, probably, but nearly two centuries later, the remark seems little creditable to Colonel Mercer. A colonel and a scion of colonial aristocracy, he should have avoided "begging, praying, beseeching, importuning, etc., etc.," as unworthy of his class and calibre. He had already begun to think of selling his Virginia assets and think in terms of raising money both in Great Britain and in Virginia by mortgages. In this letter he wrote, "You mention the difficulty you were in about fixing the price of the Shenandoah land, which from my father's letter I think very easily to be got over. Colonel Lewis, he writes me, was to purchase it." To his brother he confided that he had been appointed "a Lt. Gov." "He was appointed in 1769 to succeed Governor Tryon, who was sent to New York. But Colonel Mercer did not go to North Carolina after all and Major Martin, a British officer, became governor of that colony in 1771." [158] The *Virginia Gazette,* November 24, 1768, carried an announcement of his appointment as Lieutenant Governor of North Carolina and March 23, 1769, carried an item announcing the arrival of George Mercer "at New Bern N. C." If so, George Mercer took another dangerous and disagreeable mid-winter passage across the Atlantic. Did he really come back to America in 1769? Newspapers can be mistaken or inaccurate. Before the coming of the telegraph, the telephone, radio and television and the emergence of news agencies, such error, in journalism, was more likely than now. Mary Mercer, the second wife of George Mercer, stated later that though Colonel Mercer got the appointment to be Lieutenant Governor of North Carolina, the appointment was "without any salary or Emolument whatever, not even so much as to defray the expense of making out his Commission." In his straitened financial circumstances George Mercer could not accept appointment under such conditions.

In the autumn of 1768, October 14, John Mercer who, as stated above, was born in Dublin, February 6, 1704, came to America in 1720 and married Catherine Mason in 1726, died at Marlborough. His son George was then in Europe, was unavoidably not at his funeral and seems never to have come back to Marlborough.

One reason, very likely, why George Mercer of the Ohio Company did not become Lieutenant Governor of North Carolina was competition in London with other colonial land-grant petitioners.

Arthur Lee and fifty associates, including Presley Thornton and Thomas Ludwell Lee, members of the Ohio Company, put in a petition for a vast acreage in the Mississippi Valley,[159] and the Pennsylvania group around Thomas Walpole put in a petition in June 1769 for the territory once actually settled by the Ohio Company. On November 20, 1769, the Lords of the Committee of the Privy Council submitted George Mercer's Memorial of 1767 to the Board of Trade and Plantations for their consideration and advice.[160] But the Pennsylvania group (variously known as Suffering Traders, Walpole Company, Indiana Company, Vandalia Company and Grand Ohio Company), having received in 1768, at Fort Stanwix, large land cessions from the Indians, offered the British government £ 10,000 for much of the lands ceded by the Indians and thus secured the good will not only of the King in Council, of some in the Board of Trade and Plantations, but also of the important Treasury officials. Success for this group was so imminent that it seemed guaranteed.

The European holders of shares in the old Ohio Company, having become disillusioned or indifferent or both, George Mercer was nevertheless in late 1769 an alert watch dog of the interests of the Americans who had appointed him their agent six years earlier. On December 18, 1769, he put in a last desperate memorial, in the nature of a legal caveat. Overtly sincere, this document said, "Your memorialist . . . most humbly prays your lordships not to make any grant, within the limits prescribed by the royal instruction to the company [March 16, 1749]; as they are, and have ever been willing and desirous to proceed in their undertaking, and fulfil their engagements to government." He ends the memorial with the statement, "And that no unnecessary delay may be offered to the petitioners, on behalf of the Ohio Company, your memorialist begs leave, humbly to represent, that he is fully prepared whenever your lordships shall be pleased to command him, to justify the companys pretensions, and show, they have, through no neglect on their part, been delayed upward of twenty years, from executing a plan, which would have contributed as much to the public, as their own private interest." [161] This is a brilliant statement, based upon the study of law, acquaintance with the past facts, possession of copies of many of the documents of the company, and long experience with memorials.

George Mercer at this time had in his possession copies of many of the records of the Ohio Company. They are, probably most of them, found in the so-called George Mercer Papers and in print under that title. The Company's old London attorney, Charlton Palmer, on December 27, 1769, addressed Colonel Mercer, at Holles Street, Cavendish Square, saying, "All the papers I rec'ed except what I gave you I delivered to Mr. Jackson (who then lived in the Temple but now in Southern plan Buildings Chancery Lane) which I understood were redelivered to you." [162]

The slow moving wheels of government in London are seen in an item of the Board of Trade and Plantations of January 3, 1770, "Order of the Lords of the Committee of Council, dated November 20, 1769, referring to this board, for their consideration and report, the petition of George Mercer in behalf of the Ohio Company . . ." [163] In competition, much like a typical horse race, the so-called Vandalia Company presented its memorial to the British Treasury. [164]

On March 8, 1770, George Mercer wrote Richard Conway Dobbs, son and heir of Arthur Dobbs, an old member of the Ohio Company. He asked what had happened to the share and what disposition would be made of it. [165] A statement of the account of the Ohio Company with Arthur Dobbs was probably sent in this letter. [166] It indicated not only that more than £ 100 had not been paid, but that probably all payments had been in the form of promissory notes. George Mercer perhaps was making an effort either to collect the balance and payment of the notes with interest or else to acquire the share himself at its low market value of 1770. In his letter of reply, March 26, 1770, Dobbs made a later appointment and wrote, "It gives me Pleasure to Hear that You are appointed Lieut. Govr. of North Carolina." [167]

On March 28, 1770, George Mercer wrote to his first military commander, George Washington. [168] Probably throughout April 1770, Colonel Mercer was doubly engaged in watching the activities of Thomas Walpole, Samuel Wharton and others in what had come to be called the Grand Ohio Company, and in compiling the now famous Case of 1770. As has so well been shown in "Commentary on the Case of the Ohio Company Extracted from Original Papers" (George Mercer Papers, 393-458), some of the contents of the sixty-two page imprint came from the head and pen of George Mercer. Most of it came from Ohio Company records or materials already in his possession. It is more than a conjecture that some of the sheets may already have been printed [169] in 1767 and, with other sheets added, put out as a bound imprint in late April or early May 1770.

As far as George Mercer's agency of the Ohio Company was concerned, he had reached the end of his rope in May 1770. He was so much frustrated as to be ready to throw in the sponge of defeat. On May 7, 1770, he came to terms with the gentlemen of the Grand Ohio

Company, surrendering the old Ohio Company claims while agreeing to accept and meet the expenses of a small fractional share in the larger grant asked for and expected by the Grand Ohio Company.[170] This acknowledgment may have been logical under the circumstances, but it was nevertheless an indication of the final frustration of seven years of solicitation and of as many years of his career. On May 8, 1770, Thomas Walpole put in another petition to the King, and on the same day George Mercer transmitted a memorial, cancelling his past memorials,[171] which on May 10, 1770, was before the Board of Trade and Plantations.[172] His position in London, which from the beginning had been troublesome and questionable now became deplorable. To his unpopularity as distributor of stamps in 1765, was now to be added repudiation by the very members of the Ohio Company who had impowered him and sent him over as agent in 1763. He was likely to remain in the dark shadows of rejection, disrespect and disrepute. For a time friendly relations could be and were maintained with prominent individuals such as George Mason, Robert Carter, George Washington, and James Mercer, his brother, but one after another of these old friends became critical, pitying, scornful, and in the case of his brother, unfriendly. A letter, July 24, 1770, of George Mercer to George Mason is mentioned by the latter in a letter to an unnamed relative, December 6, 1770.[173] Mercer is reported to have spoken very doubtfully of the Ohio Company affairs and to have written that he expected to return to Virginia in September 1770.

Possibly already in the depths of frustration and despair, George Mercer, September 1, 1770, drew up a Last Will and Testament,[174] making his brother James his main heir and the executor of his estate in Virginia, but with provisions (believed to have been later voided in codicils) for two or more patrons and friends in England.

Unlike so many Last Wills, this one was not followed soon by the death of its maker. George Mercer was to live nearly fourteen years longer.

In October 1770, George Mercer seems to have sent a small packet of materials to George Mason who complained that they contained only old data. In December he made a trip to Dublin, Ireland, possibly in connection with matters mentioned by his father in his abnormally long letter of January 28, 1768. From Dublin, Colonel Mercer wrote George Washington, December 18, 1770, about the long promised military bonus lands. He mentioned his agreement with the Grand Ohio Company and, it is said, "He notified Washington that the 200,000 acres claimed by the Virginia soldiers had been accepted by the company as valid" and that these claims would be respected.[175] And he announced that he planned to go to England in a few days and then to Virginia as soon as he could.

George Mercer in 1771 still had assets and prospects. He had title to vast tracts of land in Virginia. On his plantation on the Shenandoah he had a tenant, slaves, horses and general equipment. He had claims by military service, by purchase and by inheritance from John Fenton Mercer, to nearly fifteen thousand acres of military bounty lands. He had a share in the Grand Ohio Company, as well as in the seemingly defunct Ohio Company, of Virginia. And he and his brother James thought he had claims to the extent of £ 3000 against members of the older company. There was also a rumor as late as February 7, 1771,[176] that he would be the next governor of North Carolina.

That he was in 1771 the George Mercer of old is seen in a letter to his brother James, March 27, 1771, in which he not only mentions shipping songbirds, mares and colts, but also his latest romance, saying, "I believe she is a good girl — yet I want to see a greater Parity of Sentiments between us." His financial and probably emotional distress at this time is apparent from the pages of a long and tortuous letter by him to Richard Conway Dobbs, May 28, 1771,[177] the main subject of which was the old Arthur Dobbs share in the Ohio Company.

Onset of Distress

In this letter of May 28, 1771, George Mercer revealed himself as at the lowest ebb in health, spirit and finances. As an excuse for delay and neglect in writing, he said that he had been so "torn to Pieces with the Remains of my Fever and the Beginnings of a Rheumatism, that it is but seldom I can find myself capable of doing business. Lowness of Spirits prevents me from attempting it often, and Pain of my Limbs from going through it." This is the language of a valetudinarian, not unlike his brother, James Mercer, as described by John Mercer in his letters of 1768.

George Mercer offered to buy the Dobbs share at the price of the money advanced on it, but not including any interest. In this connection he wrote that he could not bind the Ohio Company to pay for it, but said, "I will take the Risque on myself as the Company have no Right to find Fault with me for the Disposal of my own money and purchase your Share for my own Account . . ." Commenting on the Ohio Company and any letter of credit from them, he wrote, "I can not raise a Shilling here on their Credit . . . ," and mentions "near £ 1000 which I have already advanced" and that he expected "to be called on this week for upwards of £ 400 more for the Grant" (from the Grand Ohio Company). The language, even the grammar and rhetoric, of the eighteenth century is not entirely clear two centuries later and, as a result in this letter of a convalescent, shares in the two companies are not sufficiently distinguished from each other.

From the rather scanty records which have been found, it is very evident that George Mercer had risked everything on the prospects of success of the Grand Ohio Company. He boasted in a letter that no step of that Company was taken without himself being acquainted with the proceedings. Possibly this was wisdom, but his circumstances were compulsory. In debt, indeed impoverished, in low spirits, sometimes sick and in pain, the Grand Ohio Company must have seemed to him his only way out, his last hope of preferment, promotion, prosperity and success.

The letters of Mercer to Thomas Adams, an old American colonial who had become a successful London merchant, and a benefactor of needy or stranded Americans, have been in print for many years.[178] On one unfamiliar with the career of George Mercer, they produce an unfavorable impression, reminding an old Oxonian of some of the almost unbelievable situations at Oxford of some young aristocrats of similar status in England.

In one of the letters, undated but thought to be of 1771, a distressing financial situation is depicted. He writes:

My dear Adams You must by some means or other procure me £ 50 by Tuesday morning or I must go to the Dogs. The note I mentioned to you formerly falls due on that day it has already been renewed about six times, and is in the Hands of a Lawyer who has sent me word he **can't** lay out his money any longer, d—n the Fellows Conscience he has added 6 s. 8 d. for a Fee for writing to me besides interest every Time it has been renewed, and yet yesterday sent to remind me of the notes falling due with the addition I mention and that I must take up.

That he was now a drowning man grasping at a straw is seen in the next sentence, "I shall ask no more from you till Anderson [a shipmaster] arrives who I hope will bring me half a hundred puncheons of Shenandoah [tobacco] which will honestly pay all my debts."

His straitened circumstances are set forth in two last sentences as follows:

I know both you and B's poverty, and yet I cannot help, and I am sure you will both do me the Justice to believe I would not trouble you if it was possible to avoid it. If you can by any means negotiate the note I send I shall be strong enough by the time it falls due, tho' at present I give you my oath I have not a Brace of pounds in the world nor do I know where to get them unless you or Brown will help me.

65

It is only a slight defense of this revelation to point out that men of George Mercer's class and type, especially in England but also in America, have often lived unproductively and extravagantly, remaining in debt and ever chasing the pot of gold at the end of rainbows.

Another letter to Adams, from Yarmouth, August 6, 1771, reveals the same financial distress, involved with romantic adventure or adventures.[179] In the language of an editor or commentator, he was "trying to marry a young lady whose parents or guardians oppose the match." He writes:

> I am obliged to be in town on Sunday if it is possible to settle this affair beyond Doubt, but as I have two bills amounting to £ 60 which fall due on Tuesday (for fear of Disappointments) I must beg the favor of you to get me the money by Hook or by Crook for the interest Bills, and leave it with my House Keeper on Monday, as will not appear quite so decent should I be arrested on my Return Home with Madam, for such a sum as £ 60.

Acquaintance with similarly involved individuals in England and America would lead one to suspect that as roomer and boarder, Colonel Mercer had not paid his "House Keeper" for many months and possibly faced the loss of his personal property. He concludes the letter with "Adieu till we meet, dont' tell any one where I am or my Business, till I tell you the Knot is tied and you must never mention a syllable of this scuffle to Maria, as she says she shall never be able to look any one except myself in the face who knows it." As an addendum rather than as a postscript, although it follows his signature, he says as an afterthought, "I have told her [presumably the young lady with him] I am writing to a particular Friend — she desires for Heaven's Sake and for the sake of my own character, that I will not mention to him that I have a giddy hot head runaway young girl with me, especially if the friend has anything serious about him."

Whether the "Knot" was tied, and there is little proof that it was, George Mercer, on August 8, 1771, was back at his old quarters on Holles Street, Cavendish Square, London, for from that address he wrote that day a long letter to George Mason.[180] In it he discussed, first, his eight year agency for the Ohio Company and their neglect of him; secondly, the low rating of the Ohio Company in 1771; thirdly, the failure of the members to correspond with him and honor their agreement of 1763; and, fourthly, his bad financial circumstances. Among quotable phrases may be mentioned "not one word of answer . . . no money, no Credit, no approbation of my past Conduct, or orders for my future"; "I have given them Notice at least twenty times that I was half that sum [£ 2,000] in advance and have never been able to get 12 s. in Return, or even an Answer to one of my Letters"; and "The curse of dancing attendance on the ministers and public Boards I have frequently mentioned though with less than a thousandth part of the humiliating Circumstances that are forced upon the poor wretch who is obliged to cringe and ask a Favor of them." The document is doubly endorsed as "Complaining of want of Instructions and Remittances."

In the light of similar frustrations of George Croghan, William Trent, Samuel Wharton and others of the Grand Ohio Company and in view of the promises made to George Mercer in 1763, this emotional outburst is not surprising, for the failure of the old Company in the New World, as well as in the Old, has to be taken into consideration.

Another letter to the Company enclosed with the above missive was probably of the same purport. It probably reached Williamsburg, Virginia, in October and possibly was responsible for the James Mercer papers included in the *George Mercer Papers* (pp. 312-23). When Robert Carter, who was in Williamsburg, got the information found in the letter, he, on October 24, 1771, wrote George Mercer, saying he had not known the terms of George Mercer's appointment in 1763, that he had just heard of George Mercer's letter of October 10, 1767, and four other letters of that year. "I will patronize you," he said, "tho the measures have not succeeded wch you adopted." He sent Mercer permission to get, on his bond, £ 200 from Carter's London agents and said he had advised Lee and Tayloe to give Mercer further credit.[181] Much belated, this was an evidence of good will on the part of one who himself had dallied in London as a young man but it should be noticed that he required a bond. He may have realized the situation and been uncertain about George Mercer's estate in Virginia.

Resort to Mortgages

In financial desperation, Colonel Mercer, September 30, 1771, made out a mortgage deed to Richard Gravatt, covering title to 6,500 acres of land in his Shenandoah River tract in Frederick County, Virginia. Three years later this deed was sent to Virginia and recorded in the files of the General Court, but since neither the original nor its recordation have been found, it is impossible to state how much money was involved. It may well have been several thousand pounds sterling.[182] And it should not be overlooked that in 1771,

George Mercer, by bounty claims was, in 1771, allotted 13,552 acres of western land.

George Washington wrote George Mercer, November 7, 1771, saying, "Since you first left this Country, I have been favored with two letters from you, one of them dated the 28th of March 1770, the other of the 18th of December" [1770]. One sentence said frankly, "I have just been told by Mr. [James] Mercer that you remain in London for some advices from him respecting the Affairs of the Ohio Company." Only military lands policy and proceedings are found in Washington's second letter of November 22, 1771.[183]

A letter of Robert Carter to James Mercer, December 9, 1771, was mainly an excerpt of his letter of October 24, 1771, to George Mercer. But James Mercer probably took the occasion of this correspondence to put his brother's case before Carter, saying he had written each resident member of the Company, mentioning his brother's expenses and claims against the Company. James Mercer wished to know if Carter approved the agreement made by George with the Grand Ohio Company and wished a share in the agreement. If so, he hoped Carter would send him £ 200 for each two-fortieths share in the old Ohio Company he might own.[184]

It is certain that George Mercer, by February 1772, in exchange for his bond, received £ 200 from Thomas and Rowland Hume, London agents of Robert Carter.[185] Probably this money strengthened his morale and encouraged him to seek other and additional relief. On February 20, 1772, he handed in a memorial to the Earl of Hillsborough requesting some reward for his services in North America during the late war, and he accompanied it with a copy of his memorial of 1766 about his work as distributor of stamps.[186] Late in February, Robert Carter was duly notified that George Mercer had drawn the money "on signing 2 bonds (both of the same tenor and date)." [187]

Not only George Mercer himself, but some of his friends in Virginia and in England believed, at the time, in the eventual success of the Grand Ohio Company. Jonathan Boucher, the well known clergyman, so expressed himself to George Washington, March 5, 1772.[188] And Samuel Wharton, August 5, 1772, accepted a draft of Mercer upon him for £ 250. A short document, it tells much, for the things in connection with and sometimes behind statistics are frequently significant if not profound. In full the document is as follows:

68

due Novr. 5/8th
£ 250

London August the 5th 1772
Three Months after Date pay to my Order Two hundred
and fifty Pounds, Value received, as advised.
To Samuel Wharton, Esq.

Geo: Mercer
New Suffolk Street   Accepted
London   Saml. Wharton
[Endorsed:]
Geo: Mercer
Recd. Novr. 8 1772 of Samuel Wharton Esqr. the full Contents
of the within Draft.
Edwd. Blackshaw.[189]

This draft has the appearance of a payment, by its means, for
a share in the Grand Ohio Company, an item which Wharton sold
to Edward Blackshaw, but had to redeem himself on the last possible
date. But there is at least the possibility that George Mercer actually
got the £ 250 and Wharton sold the draft, but later had to redeem it.

In this same year, 1772, George Mercer gave a deed mortgage to
"Mary Wroughton, spinster of Bath." It was on some of his Virginia
lands, seemingly mainly in Fauquier County. Since it also was recorded in the General Court of Virginia and not seemingly today
extant, but only mentioned in recorded deeds of sale, November 1774,
it is, again, impossible to state the amount of mortgage money received,
though it was probably a few thousand pounds. The likelihood of
overlapping claims to George Mercer's estate necessitated appeal to
the Virginia Court of Chancery and an interlocutory decree of
November 4, 1773.

On August 20, 1772, Wharton announced to George Mercer a
belated report of the Committee of the Privy Council in favor of the
Grand Ohio Company, addressing George Mercer as still at Holles
Street, Cavendish Square. It is, therefore, not wholly astounding that
George Mercer stayed on in Europe, awaiting the outcome of
this matter.

It was in the midst of this uncertainty and expectancy in London,
that George Washington, from Mount Vernon, December 23, 1773,
announced the final distribution of military bounty land claims, a
division in which George Mercer got claims to 6,000 acres of his own
right and another 6,000 as the heir of his brother, John Fenton Mercer,
killed on the frontier in 1756.[190]

Frantic Finance

After nearly a decade abroad with no governmental employment
and with little, if any, income from more than 10,000 acres of good
land and another 15,000 acres of wilderness land from military

bounty lands, George Mercer, temporarily abroad in flight from English creditors, on November 4, 1772, turned to his old friend, William Trent, then in England, for assistance.[191]

It was in early 1772, that James Mercer tried earnestly to raise money for his brother George, by appeals to members of the old Ohio Company who had sent him over in July 1763. But, by 1772, some of the members had forgotten the circumstances. Probably few, if any, sympathized with George Mercer after his so unpremeditated long stay abroad. Some of them had been alienated by the stamp distribution episode and its resultant quarrel. And many were discomfited and aggravated by the surrender of the old Ohio Company claims by George Mercer in 1770, with the attempted merger with the Grand Ohio Company. While satisfactory contemporary documentation is lacking, it appears that James Mercer's appeals and proposals were entirely rejected.[192]

Defeated in his direct appeal to the Ohio Company for additional funds so badly needed and so strongly requested by George Mercer, James Mercer, with powers of attorney given him in 1763 and supplemented in 1765, and seemingly unaware of prior mortgages by George Mercer in England, gave, November 13, 1772, to James Hunter and Albert Dick of Fredericksburg, a mortgage deed on the land of George Mercer. Here overlapping claims were unmistakable. And since cash money was scarce and credit was almost invariably given in the acceptance of bonds, George Mercer probably did not receive, quickly, even a pittance of cash or of negotiable credit.

Another letter of George Mercer to William Trent, March 10, 1773, reveals the same but possibly more distressing financial situation. It shows Colonel Mercer arrested and thrown into prison for debt. "My Ruin," he wrote, "dear Major is at Length compleated." He stated he had ordered his "Housekeeper" to pack up his clothing and asks Trent to get it while she was away visiting "my dear little Girl Patty . . . ," at the Boarding School. The nomenclature here is vague but important. "Housekeeper" was earlier used by George Mercer as term for wedded mate. The reference to "my dear little Girl Patty" seems to have been one to Martha Mercer, daughter of Mary Neville Mercer and from birth, about 1768, a hopeless cripple. The letter closes with the exclamation, "Heavens — What . . . do I feel to see myself inclosed within strong Iron Bars . . . I cannot write more . . . my Heart is so full . . . it overflows . . ." Another short note, probably of the same day, indicates that he was again in flight to Dover and the continent.

70

At this time James Mercer began to sell slaves and negotiate for the sale of George Mercer's landed property in Fairfax County. And George Washington was then, as usual, in the market for slaves and for tracts of land near Mount Vernon. His writings reveal much attention to this, and full information about the lands may be found in old deed books of Fairfax County. On July 19, 1773, Washington wrote James Mercer for a "fresh mortgage," having neglected to have the earlier one recorded.

In this letter Washington, frankly but somewhat bluntly, said, "I have been told that both your Father's and Brother's Affairs are a good deal involved in perplexity and distress," a completely accurate impression, somewhat ameliorated by the fact that inventories of the estates of other local men, supposed to be wealthy, showed, at times, assets equivalent to less than a tenth of outstanding obligations.

George Mercer, in Europe, must have been early informed that the Board of Trade and Plantations had drawn up, May 6, 1773, a constitution for Vandalia. And soon rumors of a governorship of a western colony began to appear in American colonial newspapers. Colonel Mercer was reported to have been nominated for the position of governor of an Ohio Valley colony and, later, to have been appointed governor of Pittsylvania.[193] In 1773, he was badly in need of some position and emolument. He had mortgaged his Virginia property to Richard Gravatt and Mary Wroughton in England and, on May 15, 1773, there was sent over, as is stated in deeds of November 1774, a power of attorney, dated May 1, 1773, to John Tayloe, George Mason and George Washington to sell his Virginia estate and pay off the mortgages.[194] Also in his distress in London, George Mercer put in yet another memorial to British authorities asking some reward for his services in the army 1754-1763 and for his expenses and troubles as stamp distributor in 1765.[195]

Two significant statements about George Mercer's bad financial management and circumstances, are seen in a letter of George Mason to George Washington, December 21, 1773.[196] One of them says, "When Colo. Mercer was first married and thought in affluent circumstances by his Friends here, considerable purchases of Slaves were made for him at high prices (and I believe mostly upon Credit) which must now be sold at much less than the cost." Since only his brother, James Mercer, had then the power of attorney for George Mercer, this is a criticism, however indirect and gentle, of James Mercer, and this transaction may well have been responsible for the later unfriendliness between the brothers, a trouble deplored by George

71

Washington who endeavored to ameliorate and, if possible, end the bad situation.

The second statement is, "He was originally burthened wth. a proportionable part of his Father's Debts, most of which as well as the old Gentleman's other Debts, are not only still unpaid, but must be greatly increased by Interest so that, even if Colo. Mercer had not incurred a large Debt in England, He would have found his Affairs here in a disagreeable Situation." Probably the bond of November, 1759, if actually negotiated, had not yet been satisfied and evidently George Mason was cognizant of George Mercer's situation in London. The remainder of the letter deals with George Mercer's tracts "on Polick Run and on Four-mile Run in Fairfax County," some or all of which were later acquired by George Washington.

George Mercer, in early 1774, must have written George Washington again about the sale of his Virginia lands, for Washington wrote to this purport, March 28, 1774, saying, ". . . Colo. Mercer, of all things . . . desires a speedy Sale of his Land etc., that the Mortgages may be satisfied, let his suffering, under it, be as it will, expecting, on this occasion, to encounter considerable loss." [197] The letter giving Tayloe, Mason and Washington powers of attorney inevitably became known and was given publicity in the newspaper.[198] In April 1774, George Mercer was seen in London by Captain Robert Mackenzie who mentioned him in a letter from Boston to George Washington, September 13, 1774,[199] saying he had a detail of grievances but his health and spirit seemed to have suffered little.

In the late summer, August 6, 1774, George Mercer wrote a long letter to Robert Carter, enclosing copies of the *Case* of the Grand Ohio Company, complaining of the old Ohio Company's neglect of him, upholding his agreement of 1770, and flattering the prospects of the Grand Ohio Company.[200] He did not know that two weeks earlier, Robert Carter had written John Taswell [*sic*] about Mercer's bonds of 1771 and had inquired about his estate with a view probably of attaching some part of it as repayment.

Political Principles

An undetermined matter is that of George Mercer's interest in imperial and colonial politics. There is found no evidence of such profound analysis of factors as appears in the writings of George Mason and others. It may be that George Mercer approved the lull in the storm of imperial-colonial relations 1770 to 1774. But it is hard to understand how he could be unaware of the renewal of discord with the Tea Act of 1773, the opposition to it in the American colonies and the break in amity caused by tea parties in Boston and elsewhere in 1774. Samuel Wharton saw the handwriting on the wall, the doom of further royal grants and eventually returned to Philadelphia. It would seem that George Mercer made another blunder when he failed to leave London in 1774 and return to Virginia before his estate had been sold at public auction in November 1774. Bad as his credit was at that stage, both in the New World and in the Old, he might have bid in for some of his holding and saved himself considerable money. It seems highly probable that he was so much and in so many ways involved in England that he could not get away without loss of his own self-respect as well as the respect of others. Possibly he was at heart an imperialist or imperial unionist. His father was born and reared in Dublin, Ireland, then in the English Pale. George had relatives there with whom he was in contact for more than a decade, staying at times with them on extended visits. And from 1757 his contacts with British military figures such as Bouquet, Forbes, Stanwix, Monckton and Amherst were frequent and close. In addition he was from 1763 in touch with high imperial officials in London. He may have been a loyalist in principle as was stated in various petitions and letters which have survived. His seeming sycophancy had at least a veneer of principle.

It was widely known that George Mercer's Virginia assets would be up for sale in November 1774. William Crawford, writing George Washington from the Ohio Valley, November 14, 1774, stated that "... when Those Negroes of Mercer's are Sold and they are Sold at Credit (12 months) I would be Glad to Purchase a boy and Girl about 14 or 15 years old Each or older if Such are Sold." [201] Since George Mason, by reason of kinship, declined to serve, and John Tayloe neglected his responsibility, the entire burden of this sale fell upon the gentleman from Mount Vernon.

Writing to Captain Robert Mackenzie, October 9, 1774, Washington remarked sympathetically, "poor Mercer! I often hear from him; much cause has he, I fear, to lament his having fallen into the accursed state of attendance and dependence," [202] a statement which hit the nail on the head. Others, referring to George Mercer, were to use this same adjective "poor," which really had a double meaning.

Sale of Estate, 1774

Soon after the Interlocutory Decree of November 5, 1773, items about the sale of George Mercer's estate began to appear in the newspapers.[203] Washington, in a legal paper many years later, February

73

15, 1789, claimed the sale was well advertised.[204] Probably posters were also printed and circulated as was customary then and later. They, or other statements, may have been displayed on court days at the courthouses of Fauquier and Frederick counties. It is probable that, as in Frederick County, a survey of the entire George Mercer tract, in Fauquier County, was made in October 1774. The survey probably included a plat and separate surveys of individual lots to be sold. Since it is not recorded in Fauquier County, it is not impossible that it is a part of the plat of twenty-two surveys later filed and recorded in Frederick County, though it may have been lost or recorded in the Virginia land-office.

George Washington either had an able lawyer with him immediately to write bonds, and possibly deeds, or he had prepared forms for each of the parcels of land. He appears to have gone first to Fauquier County, where he began individual sales on November 21, 1774. The deeds given were unusually complex, for they ran in the names of George Mercer . . . Mary Wroughton . . . John Tayloe and George Washington, all of whose signatures had to be secured after identification of the indenture and of the signatures, before it could be recorded. In some cases recordation was long delayed. Eight of the deeds were made out on November 21, 1774, and, here highly abbreviated, were: To John Peyton Harrison, 306 acres for £ 132 (Deed Book 6, f. 117) ; to John Monday, 470 acres for £ 99 (*Ibid.*, f. 120) ; to George Sullivan, 522 acres for £ 355 (*Ibid.*, f. 135) ; to Peter Bryant, 100 acres for £ 81 (*Ibid.*, f. 138) ; to William Owen, 120¾ acres for £ 111 (*Ibid.*, f. 140) ; to Owen Powell, 184 acres for £ 40 (*Ibid.*, 10, f. 127) ; to William Pickett Sanford, 358 acres for £ 200 (*Ibid.*, 10, f. 129) ; to Nathaniel and Cornelius Skinner, 1057 acres (Bull Run Mountain) for £ 61 (*Ibid.*, 15, f. 248). A later deed of November 30, 1774, was to James Lewis, 139 acres for £ 61 (*Ibid.*, 13, f. 144), or a total of 3256¾ acres, for £ 1,140 Virginia currency, or about seven shillings per acre.

After the Fauquier County sales, George Washington, the acting attorney-in-fact for George Mercer and his creditors, proceeded to Frederick County where in the last week of November he sold to the highest bidders, the property of George Mercer in that jurisdiction. Recorded are the sales: To Thomas Berry, 357 acres for £ 221 (Deed Book 16, f. 636) ; to Benjamin Berry, 560 acres for £ 270 (*Ibid.*, f. 642) ; to Colin Campbell, 235 acres for £ 127 (*Ibid.*, 17, f. 1-4) ; to George Noble, 650 acres for £ 493 (*Ibid.*, f. 4) ; and to Francis Willis, (blank) for £ 632 (*Ibid.*, 18, f. 681). In addition must be mentioned as found recorded, 320 acres sold to Fielding Lewis for £ 322, and 591 acres, not found recorded, to George Washington and James Mercer. This superior Shenandoah Valley land seems to have sold for a price averaging about twelve shillings per acre.

In addition, George Mercer's slaves, horses, cattle, farm implements, etc., were sold. Those in Fauquier and Frederick counties who bought on bonds numbered at least forty-four. The total paid for land seems to have been about £ 3,796. The slaves, live stock, implements and crops probably increased the total to about £ 6,000. A potential estate of great future possibilities thus fell under the hammer of some auctioneer, and was scattered under many holders.

In writing about the sales, George Washington, November 30, 1774, informed John Tayloe, his inactive fellow attorney-in-fact for George Mercer, "We closed the matter this day to the amount of £ 1412.0.2, which is a greater Sale than I expected, as there were only 90 instead of 110 Negroes and a proportionate deficiency of Horse and Stock; and few or no Plantation utensils." [205] It may well be that £ 1412.0.2 was only for these items found on the plantation in Frederick County, for Washington added, "the land in this County (that is, Frederick) sold for much less than it was valued at in the year 1767; and yet I do not think it sold much under the intrinsic worth as there is a good deal of exceeding poor and broken ground in it." But, as stated above, Washington himself bought some of the land, Lots 5 and 6, totaling 591 acres.

Other property of George Mercer seems to have been sold in the same period. In the manuscript papers of George Washington is a deed of sale by George Mercer and others to George Washington of 1,168 acres of land on Four Mile Run, Fairfax County, Virginia, for £ 900. It is signed by George Mercer, James Mercer and two others and endorsed as proved before a General Court, April 15, 1775. There also is a photostat of Rough Field Notes taken by George Washington in running the sources of land bought from George and James Mercer. The undated field notes probably date from the winter of 1774-1775. To James Mercer, Washington wrote, December 12, 1774, ". . . enclosed you have my Bond . . . for £ 450 for your Brother's moity in the four mile run Land [in Fairfax County] as also receipts £ 40-11.11 the balance due him on account of the Ohio Lands under the Proclamation of 1754." [206]

Exactly two weeks later Washington wrote James Mercer, "the whole of your purchases in Frederick amounted to £ 2385.14.2." [207]

He added, "I have wrote to your Brother since I came home," and, though the letter has not been found, it presumably reported the results of the sales of November 1774 in Fauquier and Frederick counties.

In a long letter to Edward Montague, a Virginia agent in London, Washington, April 5, 1775, discussed many matters relating to George Mercer, whose friend, Montague, probably passed its contents on to Colonel Mercer. Washington mentioned the discord between George and James Mercer, the overlapping mortgages and powers of attorney, and stated, "That Colo. Mercer has been a considerable loser in the management of his Estate here, nobody will deny." [208]

As indicated in the bond of George Mercer to William Trent, April 14, 1775, George Mercer on that date resided at Curzon Street in the "Parish of Saint George and County of Middlesex." On April 18, 1775, the day before the conflict at Lexington and Concord, Washington again wrote George Mercer.[209]

William Trent, who himself was in London, in bad financial circumstances, but had nevertheless advanced money to George Mercer,[210] hearing about the sales of November 1774, wrote Washington, August 4, 1775, to learn if he could expect any payment out of the proceeds. Evidently he was dubious about the prospects of settlement of the penal bond of £ 400. Washington's reply was not cheerful. "His Estate . . . ," Washington reported, "sold for upwards of £ 14000 and was thought scarce sufficient to answer the Mortgages upon it in England and America; it was sold at 12 months Credit in November last, so that no money will be due till next Novr." [211] Not only George Mercer himself, but his many creditors could get no money in early 1775, and with the outbreak of the War of American Independence in April 1775, probably would not get it for some time, if ever.

Imperial Choice

As suggested above, Colonel Mercer made a bad blunder in not returning to Virginia in the summer of 1774. He blundered again by not returning as Franklin and others did on the outbreak of war, whether looked upon as revolution as in America, or as rebellion as in official circles in London. But, his Virginia estate first mortgaged and then liquidated, Colonel Mercer now turned to the British government for rescue. He put in again an application for reward for his expenses and services in connection with the Stamp Act of 1765.[212] He put in an elaborate account to the Treasury. It throws much light on the episode of 1765 and on George Mercer himself. Dated November 28, 1775, the account contains sixteen items, each of them significant. Abbreviated here, they were: Attending at the Stamp Office from the 6th of April to August 29, £ 200 - -; bonds for security 22-1-0; iron chests for stamps, 6-6-0; stationery 105 - -; two clerks and passage 70 - -; office at Williamsburg 70 - -; alterations in his house at Fredericksburg 140 - -; travelling in Virginia (588 miles) 29-8-; expresses 12 - -; sloops 30 - -; return passage 40 - -; travel from Milford Haven to London 21-9-5; attendance upon Parliament 55 days 166-13-4; a year's salary for 2 clerks 150 - -; three year contract with the clerks 60 - - -; articles not recollected 30-5-8, a total of £ 1131-14-0. In the document he mentions having already sent his papers back to Virginia, an important fact in the provenance of most of the so-called George Mercer Papers, which may not be, therefore merely what he had retained in London, at the time of his death in April 1784, for all but two of the papers antedate 1775.

A striking financial aspect of this old Stamp Act account is that the total sum so anxiously sought was less than a tenth, probably, of the mortgages he had placed on his Virginia estate and still less of the gross net sales of the property.[213]

Highly valuable biographical information is found in a letter of Colonel Mercer, December 22, 1775, to a Treasury official,[214] a letter in which he mentions ". . . the present situation of my Affairs." He claimed that promises made to him since his Application of September, "have detained me here from that Time; and though I had twice absolutely engaged a Passage to Virginia, in the last Ship great Part of my Baggage, my purpose was changed by assurances of immediate Relief." He adds, "But the cruel Disappointments and Delays I have met with have reduced me to the last Extremity and I must go with the Pacquet tomorrow unless I am assisted by Government." His address was given as "Mrs. McCleods Gardens." He reiterated his old stamp distributor account of 1765-1766, and begged for at least a part payment on it. "This Sir with the quarterly Allowance Lord North proposed to give me," he wrote, "will enable me to face my Enemies and to live free from their Persecution. If this can be granted me, I know you will tell me so, and if it can not I beseech you dear Sir 1st to let me know it immediately, that I may take Advantage of the Pacquet Boat bound to Virginia." This letter, especially the discussion of persecution, implies that what Washington sagely had called "attendance and dependence," added to debts, had finally produced a bad emotional state on Colonel Mercer's part, as early as 1775.

George Mercer, both literally and figuratively, "missed the boat" in 1775. A statement of his account with the Grand Ohio Company handed or sent him by Thomas Walpole, February 26, 1776,[215] was duly endorsed by Colonel Mercer. On March 22, 1776, he wrote John Robinson, of the Treasury, a short revealing note, saying, "I am compelled to trouble you again. I need not remind you that my Account has been ten years at the Treasury, but I do assure you on my Honour that since Lord North was pleased to promise my Business should be settled in a few days, I have expended above a fourth Part of the Amount of my original Claim on Government," adding, ". . . I have lived above six months open to every Charge that Suspense could draw me into. For Heavens Sake Sir, relieve me from this cruel and expensive State! You will ever find me grateful."[216]

It was at this time that Thomas Pownall consulted George Mercer about American wild rye, obtained an excellent statement about it from Mercer and dubbed him Lieutenant Governor Mercer.

Confused Status and Distress

After the Declaration of Independence by the United States of America, George Mercer occupied the embarrassing position of a hanger-on of a government with which his native land, now organized as a nation, was at war. This embarrassment superimposed on other hardships, was possibly responsible for his letter of August 1, 1776, to a British Lord (probably Germain), saying, "As it is impossible for me to live in England on the Generosity of Government, the only Subsistence I can at present expect, I shall be forced to use the Indulgence your Lordship was pleased to grant me, to retire to the Continent." He said he would leave London the next Tuesday. There is no unmistakable evidence of secret service activity in his remarks, "[I] shall think myself happy if I can be useful to your Lordship in the Execution of any Commands" and, "My Lord I do most humbly recommend myself to your protection; and I take the Liberty to assure you, that in whatever Sphere your Lordship shall permit me to move, my chief Study will be to merit your Approbation."[217] It would seem that he anticipated the necessity of making contact with Lord Stormont, the British Ambassador to France, for he asked a letter of introduction to him.

An expatriate from his native America, and now an exile from Great Britain, George Mercer, in August 1776, took up residence in Paris, France. It is somewhat mysterious that he at that time was on the payroll of the British Government. From Paris, where he did not escape the notice of Silas Deane, of the Lees and of the Franklins, he wrote, June 3, 1777, a typical letter to his old Lord [Germain].[218]

In this greatly revealing letter he said, "I beg your Lordships Permission to remove to Plombieres, as the Faculty [Doctors of that day were commonly called 'gentlemen of the Faculty'] have recommended those waters to me," and followed this in the typical style of one in his circumstances saying, "I have written to Lord North, requesting his Lordship will enable me to undertake and support the Journey by advancing me a Sum of Money, and at the same time I have petitioned his Lordship to increase my Allowance, which is at present, as I am informed by very good Authority, much lower than that of any Attorney General of the American provinces who certainly are inferior Officers to the Lieutenant Governors; . . . ," a statement which causes American posterity some misgivings. He admits being a pensioner; he thinks of the then independent states of the United States as provinces and of British-appointed Attorney-Generals and Lieutenant Governors as potential political realities in America, and he implies that, at the time, he was a duly appointed Lieutenant Governor. The last part of the letter contains now familiar but nevertheless remarkable data. He hoped his "Requests" for a lump sum and an increased allowance would be thought reasonable for two stated reasons: ". . . I recollect that Government has been indebted to me near twelve years a larger Sum than that I pray his Lordship to lend me" and ". . . I undertake too to repay it when Affairs in America are settled, and I am allowed to repossess my Property there . . ." One wonders, but does not know, what settlement of "Affairs in America" he had in mind. It would seem from the last half of the statement of this reason that he envisioned forced restitution of the empire. Probably his circumstances and the position of the one addressed made this statement necessary. But his remark about repossessing his property in Virginia cannot be condoned. He was not politically but voluntarily and legally dispossessed of his estate. He had really spent it in England; and the thought of retaking it was both illegal and immoral. A possible excuse is found in his statement, "Without these Aids . . . it will be impossible for me to quit Paris, as my miserable State of Health has forced me already to run into Debt." It should not be forgotten that the outbreak of war had prevented any money for him being sent from Virginia.

The printed letters of Edward Bancroft, Arthur Lee and Silas Deane reveal contemporary allegations that George Mercer in 1776 was dubbed Lieutenant Governor of North Carolina, granted an annuity or pension of £ 400 per annum and suspected of being sent to France to watch and report upon the secret activities of American agents and French politicians. Only the historical disrepute of his critics saves Colonel Mercer from severe criticism and some condemnation by posterity.

George Mercer was probably in France when Samuel Wharton, winding up the affairs of the Grand Ohio Company in London, drew up, July 17, 1777, a statement of George Mercer's Account with the Grand Ohio Company.[219] Information about him in the last seven years of his life is very scanty. He did write George Mason, April 23, 1778, but the letter has not been found but only mentioned.[220] In his reply, mainly about the American Revolution and about politics, Mason said he had not heard from Mercer or of him for two years. At the time Mason was heavily engaged in securing if possible 200,000 acres surveyed for the old Ohio Company in Kentucky in the summer of 1775. He mentions it, partly no doubt out of his interest at the time, but also as a statement of prospects of shareholders like George Mercer. He may have mentioned it as a ray of light for his relative stranded abroad and so badly frustrated.

George Mercer continued writing to American friends. On September 15, 1779, in the midst of the war, General Washington wrote Joseph Wharton,[221] "Your favor of the 25th Ulto. from Philadelphia came safe to my hands a few days ago, as did the letters you were so obliging as to bring from my old acquaintance and friend Colo. Mercer." (Mercer's letters not found.) At this late date Washington paid tribute to him as "A Gentln. for whom I always had a sincere regard." More cautiously, he wrote, "What walk of life he has been in the last four or five years and what line of conduct he has *observed* in this great contest I am totally *uninformed* of, but from the opinion I entertain of his honor, his justice, and his love to this country I would feign hope that it has been altogether unexceptionable," a statement of great generosity, worthy of its author.

Last Years

The life of George Mercer, 1780-1784, is not fully revealed by any evidence as yet found. A letter, October 13, 1780, of Silas Deane, himself discredited and in exile in Paris, says, "Sir, Yours of the 8th I received last evening," implication that at the time George Mercer was back again in London. But a letter of Le Grand de Costelle to Franklin, November 2, 1781, asked his "advice as to removing his friend, Col. George Mercer of America, who is ill in a French inn," [222]

80

supposing that an order from Congress was necessary.

The year intervening between these two letters must have been decisive for George Mercer. In disregard of the French alliance in war, he seems to have returned to France in 1781 and became a problem of Benjamin Franklin. The petition of his second wife, March 25, 1784, states flatly that reason forsook him in 1781. His illness at the French inn was probably mental as well as physical.

Without further documentary evidence, it is impossible, nearly two hundred years later, to more than imagine what must have been his confused condition, when Virginia was harassed by British troops, 1780-1781. By the last of October 1781 he was probably insane and unaffected by the surrender of Cornwallis at Yorktown. It is known that while he retained his 1776 annuity of £ 400 per year until 1782 this was reduced by £ 100 in 1782. This pension was not enough to maintain a sick insane man, his second wife and a crippled daughter in the style once maintained by George Mercer, though it should not be ignored that Loyalists such as Joseph Galloway were awarded a pension of only £ 200.

George Mercer died in London, England, in April 1784.[223] At the time of his death he still owned certain small parcels of land in Virginia. They were under the control of his brother James Mercer as his attorney-in-fact. Also it was established that in case of the intestacy of George Mercer, James Mercer, as his heir, would inherit these parcels of land.

But George Mercer was known to have made out his will in London, September 1, 1770. A copy of this old will, not attested, nor probated, nor recorded, was in the possession of James Mercer, having doubtless been sent him earlier from London. It was said in 1786 the parcels of land "yield no profit, being unimproved, and were subject to certain loss for public taxes." [224] And an act of the legislature was passed that year, for vesting in James Mercer, Esq. "certain lands whereof George Mercer died seized." [225] James Mercer was by the Act, required to enter into bond with sufficient security, to be approved by the corporation court of the Town of Fredericksburg in such penal sum as the said court shall direct.[226] The bond had to be recorded. And provision was enjoined for "a certificate for obtaining administration on the personal estate of George Mercer deceased[227] . . . the said court taking bond and security as in ordinary cases." A proviso stated that the law was to be void if the original will was located, proved and recorded.

Very unfortunately, intensive research in the records of Fredericksburg and of Spotsylvania County, Virginia, has disclosed no further light on George Mercer's estate, real or personal. No copies of the Will of 1770 nor of its codicils, no record of the bond prescribed by law, no inventories of the estate as administered, 1786-1792, could be found where expected. But a few items about the once large estate of George Mercer are found in documents of the two decades after his death. James Mercer, January 30, 1787, wrote his half-brother, John Francis Mercer, a vague letter about it, saying "the matter is unsettled for years." [228] Colonel Charles Simms of Fredericksburg called on George Washington, October 29, 1788, "respecting the affairs of Colo. Geo. Mercer and his mortgages, but Washington disclaimed any further responsibility." [229]

George Washington put out a "Statement of Facts," February 1, 1789.[230] Two weeks later he put out his answer to a bill of William Owens against him.[231] In his last will of May 23, 1791, James Mercer left to his executors, "the Trusts reposed in me by the Act of Assembly respecting my late Brother, George Mercer." [232] The signatures completing the deed of November 24, 1774, to Francis Willis, Jr., were not completed and the deed recorded, until February 6, 1793.[233] The Richard Gravatt mortgage of 1771 was not recorded in Frederick County, Virginia, until October 10, 1803.[234] John Francis Mercer, as late as February 6, 1804,[235] was writing to Alexander White and Charles Simms about bonds given at the sales of 1774, and Charles Fenton Mercer, son of James Mercer, wrote John Francis Mercer, March 30, 1805, about compromises to be negotiated with the old creditors of George Mercer in England. It is in fact impossible to say when the final settlement of the affairs of George Mercer was reached.

An Estimate

The life of George Mercer was unique mainly in three respects. He was closely related to the Ohio Company and was the instrumentality through which many important documents were preserved, a fact which of itself justifies a short accompanying biography. He unwisely became a distributor of stamps in 1765 and his later career illustrates the penalty of the mistake. Unlike most others he remained abroad and became an expatriate. Possibly more important was the matter of types of which George Mercer was a well documented illustration. Like other American colonials he was an extravagant aristocrat. Throughout his life he lived beyond the family means and his personal income, as did, however, many of his more staid and serious contemporaries.

As was the case with many tidewater Virginia gentlemen, George

82

Mercer was an accumulator and manipulator of landholdings. But here, as elsewhere, he was a user of wealth, not a creator of additional values and not an earner of profits or over-all net income. Like many of his friends and associates, George Mercer was restless, fond of change and enamored of travel. Town life and its culture appealed to him. He and many others were allured by European travel and residence, but where most of them were merely captivated, George Mercer may be said to have been actually captured rather than merely attracted.

The career of George Mercer may be explicable. That it was one featured by frequent frustrations was then and still can be clearly seen. And it is equally apparent that it ended in complete and final frustration, with mental and physical breakdown as feature or result. Some of all this seems to have been avoidable. It may be that one value of his biography is that of indication to posterity of how inimical to a successful life and career are certain ideals and policies.

The historical biographer cannot wisely depart from the factuality of the documented record. But a measure of imagination may well be added. In places in this sketch it has been suggested that ideals, decisions and events might have been otherwise. If one waive the matter of determinism and conjectures that his mental state was a result as well as a factor it is possible to imagine and picture a career far different for George Mercer than that actually revealed by documentary evidence. The things which George Mercer conceivably might have done, and possibly should have done but actually did not do, are numerous.

George Mercer might have pursued the study and practice of law. John Mercer, James Mercer and John Francis Mercer did this. George Mercer, if it had been necessary, might have as a lawyer settled down along the Blue Ridge Mountains after the manner of Gabriel Jones or in distant Kentucky, as did Henry Clay.

As already indicated, earlier above, George Mercer might have followed the career of a surveyor, architect or builder, whether in tidewater Virginia or in the up country. And he might have assumed the management of the real estate of his overworked father and possibly saved the family fortunes. In any of these three cases he might have avoided rambling around and might have married some worthy colonial girl such as the daughter of James Wood of Winchester whose husband Lawrence Augustine Washington left to her, and to posterity, an incomparable tribute. And George Mercer might well have lived less well at all times and particularly might have avoided his economically artificial life abroad.

83

George Mercer also might well have settled after 1759, on his Shenandoah plantation. Had he surrendered more quickly his position under Bouquet and Stanwix, he might not have made the significant change from America to Europe in 1763. Then he would have escaped the discredit of the stamp distribution episode. He might have stayed in Virginia in and after 1765, or he might well have returned home after the repeal of the Stamp Act in 1766. He might well also have come back to Virginia after his marriage of August 1767 and established a home on the Shenandoah. Possibly he might have avoided the agreement with the Grand Ohio Company in 1770. Financially at least he should have come back home in 1770 to superintend the affairs of his then extensive estate. The logic of his return after the Boston Tea Party of 1773 may not have impressed him, but seems today beyond serious question. More certainly he should, it seems, have returned to Virginia on the outbreak of war in 1775.

Had George Mercer done some one or more of the things here imagined and suggested, he might, as indicated above, have gone into the military service of the United States and risen to high rank. If he perchance should have survived the war, he might have settled down in old age in either Virginia or Kentucky and left to history a career of honor and distinction. It is not impossible that under such circumstances he might have lived to a ripe old age and not died abroad at the early age of fifty, after eighteen years of trouble and worry and three years of mental and physical collapse.

NOTES

1 *George Mercer Papers, Relating to the Ohio Company of Virginia.* Compiled and Edited by Lois Mulkearn, University of Pittsburgh Press, 1954 (hereinafter cited as *G. M. P.*), 204.

2 Found in the W. Garnett Chisolm Collection, Virginia Historical Society, Richmond, Virginia.

3 The fact of his attendance was attested by authorities at William and Mary College in 1958, but on the basis of very inadequate institutional information.

4 Upon Map No. 45, in Series I, Vol. I of Archer Butler Hulbert's Crown Collection of Photographs of American Maps. An excellent old re-draft of this map is found in *G. M. P.,* opp. p. 226.

5 *G. M. P.,* 52-54; 176; and 269-71.

6 *Ibid.,* 147-150; 178-79.

7 *Ibid.,* 227. The surviving copy, in the Crown Collection, is obviously not that once in the possession of John Mercer, but probably yet a third copy submitted to what George Mercer was accustomed to call "The Government." It was in the Public Record office in 1882, very likely in the Treasury papers, for in 1769 copies of some of the Ohio Company papers were deposited with the Treasury.

8 George Washington. *The Writings of . . . From the Original Manuscript Sources, 1745-1795.* John C. Fitzpatrick, ed. Washington, Government Printing Office (1931-44), 39 vols. (hereinafter cited as *G. W.*), I, 78.

9 Virginia. General Assembly, House of Burgesses. *Journal of . . .* 1752-58, 198 (hereinafter cited as *Journal of House of Burgesses*).

10 Kate Mason Rowland. *Life of George Mason,* I, 77-78 (hereinafter cited as Rowland, *Mason*). See the deed, from the Alexandria Trustees to George Mercer, September 9, 1754, Deed Book C 1, folio 794, Fairfax County, Virginia. He probably sold it to John Askon, November 20, 1754, *ibid.,* folio 842.

11 George Washington. *The Writings of,* I, 185.

12 Disney, Orderly Book, Library of Congress MS.; Lowdermilk, *History of Cumberland,* 278.

13 Pennsylvania Historical Society, *Memoirs,* V, 363-64.

14 Douglas S. Freeman. *George Washington,* Charles Scribner's Sons, New York, 1948-date, 4 vols. (hereinafter cited as Freeman, *Washington*), II, 130.

15 *Dinwiddie Papers,* II, 315-17; *G. W.,* I, 288.

16 *G. W.,* I, 518.

17 *Ibid.,* 530-531; Freeman, *Washington,* II, 231.

18 *Ibid.,* I, 530.

19 *Ibid.,* II, 20.

20 Mentioned in *Journal of House of Burgesses,* 488.

21 *G. W.,* II, 36; *Letters to Washington.* Ed. S. M. Hamilton, II, 78-81 (hereinafter cited as *Letters to G. W.*).

22 *G. W.,* II, 86.

23 *Henry Bouquet. The Papers of . . .* Originals in British Museum, Additional Manuscripts. Photostats in Library of Congress (hereinafter cited as *B. P.,* with British Museum number and folio), 21,631 folio 20 Df.

24 *Letters to G. W.,* II, 173-180.

25 *B. P.,* 21,631, folio 63.

26 *Letters to G. W.,* II, 226-28.

27 *B. P.,* 21,632, folio 20 A.

28 *Ibid.,* folio 21 B.

29 *G. W.,* II, 183-85.

30 *Ibid.,* 203-204. This troop was put under Captain Robert Stewart. Pennsylvania had, earlier, a similar light horse troop.

31 *B. P.,* 21,639, folio 17 A, A.L.S.

32 *Letters to G. W.,* II, 231.

33 *B. P.,* 21,643, folio 143, A.L.S. Bouquet in writing about Colonel Byrd, June 3, 1758, said "Lt. Col. Mercer is a Man that he can depend upon for the Command of his Regiment." *Ibid.,* 21,639, f. 9.

34 *G. W.,* II, 232-33; *B. P.,* 21,641, folio 8, A.L.S.

35 MSS Papers of Washington, VIII, folio 130, A.L.S.

36 *Letters to G. W.,* II, 355-56.

37 *Ibid.*

38 *G. W.,* II, 235; *B. P.,* 21,641, folio 11, A.L.S.

39 *Letters to G. W.,* II, 395; MSS Papers of Washington, VIII, folio 180, A.L.S.

40 *G. W.,* II, 286.

41 Orderly Book of General Forbes, Washington Papers, Library of Congress, Division of Manuscripts (hereinafter cited as Forbes Orderly Book).

42 *Journal of the House of Burgesses,* 1751-1758, 179.

43 Forbes Orderly Book, Washington Papers, L.C.

44 General John Forbes. *Writings Related to his Services in North America.* Compiled and edited by Alfred P. James, Pittsburgh, 1938 (hereinafter cited as *Forbes Writings*), 263.

45 *Journal of the House of Burgesses,* 1758-1761, 266-67.

46 *Archives of Maryland,* IX, *Correspondence of . . . Sharpe,* Vol. II, 1757-1761, 331.

47 *B. P.,* 21,644, folio 302, A.L.S.

48 *Ibid.,* 21,652, folio 148.

49 *Ibid.,* folio 149.

50 Bouquet to Thomas Walker, October 25, 1759, *B. P.,* 21,652, folio 192, A.L.S.

51 *Ibid.,* 21,644, folio 330, A.L.S.

52 *Ibid.*

53 *Ibid.,* 21,652, folio 162 A.

54 *Ibid.,* 21,644, folio 417.

55 *Letters to G. W.,* III, 158-63.

56 *B. P.,* 21,652, folio 185 C.

57 *Ibid.,* 21,644, folio 432, A.L.S.

58 *Ibid.,* 21,652, folio 189 C.

59 *Ibid.,* 21,653, folio 195.

60 Shippen Papers, Historical Society of Pennsylvania, IV, 175, A.L.S.

61 Bouquet to Mercer, October 25, 1759, *B. P.,* 21,652, folio 192, A. Df. S.

62 Mercer to Galbraith, October 22, 1759, *B. P.,* 21,644, folio 455 and Galbraith to Mercer, October 22, 1759. *B. P.,* 21,644, folio 468.

63 *B. P.,* 21,644, folio 460, A.L.S.

64 *Ibid.*

65 *Ibid.,* 21,644, folio 464, A.L.S.

66 *Ibid.,* folio 494.

67 *G. M. P.,* 40-45.

68 Mercer to Bouquet, November 28, 1759, *B. P.,* 21,644, folio 494.

69 Minutes of William and Mary College, *William and Mary College Quarterly,* first series, III, 129.

70 *B. P.,* 21,645, folio 26, A.L.S.

71 *Letters to G. W.,* III, 172-75.

72 *B. P.,* 21,645, folio 65, A.L.S.

73 *The Diaries* of George Washington. J. C. Fitzpatrick, ed. Boston, Houghton Mifflin Co., 1925, 4 vols., I, 163.

74 *B. P.,* 21,654, folio 183, A.L.S.

75 *Md. Arch.,* IX, 422-23.

76 Mercer to Trent, November 8, 1760, Historical Society of Pennsylvania, Etting Collection, Ohio Company Papers, A.L.S.

77 *B. P.,* 21,645, folios 340-51, A.L.S.

78 *Ibid.,* folio 163.

79 *Virginia Magazine of History and Biography,* LX, 411.

80 *B. P.,* 21,647, folio 72, A.L.S.

81 *Ibid.,* folio 73, A.L.S.

82 *P.R.O. W.O.* 34: 44.

83 *Journal of the House of Burgesses,* 1762, 41-42.

84 *B. P.,* 21,648, folio 160, A.L.S.

85 *Ibid.,* folio 181, A.L.S.

86 *Ibid.,* folio 181.

87 Rowland, *Mason,* I, 189.

88 See Mercer to Bouquet, August 12, 1762, *B. P.,* 21,648, folio 307, A.L.S.

89 *Ibid.,* folio 168, A.L.S.

90 *Ibid.,* folio 213, A.L.S.

91 *Ibid.,* folio 307, A.L.S.

92 *Ibid.*

93 *Ibid.,* folio 391, A.L.S. Ourry Park may have been a fanciful name for the General's House (or Commandant's House) above the fort. This house was occupied by Ourry for about five years. Ourry had a land warrant for 200 acres on Clarks Run but it was never surveyed nor patented.

94 *Journal of the House of Burgesses,* 63; 148; 152; 154; 160; 162.

95 *Ibid.,* 139.

96 *Ibid.,* 146.

97 *Ibid.,* 160.

98 *B. P.,* 21,649, f. 13, A.L.S.

99 *Ibid.,* f. 38, A.L.S.

100 *Ibid.*

101 Bouquet to General Robert Monckton, February 12, 1763, *B. P.,* 21,634, f. 206 df.

102 *The Ohio Company, Its Inner History,* by Alfred P. James, 205-219.

103 *G. M. P.,* 181-82.

104 The *Case,* in reduced facsimile, in *G. M. P.* as Part II.

105 *B. P.,* 21,634, f. 220 Df.

106 *Ibid.,* 21,649, f. 101, A.L.S.

107 *Ibid.,* 21,634, f. 244 L.S.

108 *Case, loc. cit.,* 29.

109 Deeds, Liber H, folio 350.

110 *Journal of the House of Burgesses,* May 24, 1763, 169.

111 *B. P.,* 21,649, f. 163, A.L.S.

112 *Letters to G. W.,* III, 158-63.

113 Printed in *Virginia Magazine of History and Biography,* LX, 410.

114 *Ibid.,* 350.

115 P.R.O. C.O. 5: 1331/421-30. Printed also in the *Case* of 1770, 30-31.

116 N.Y.P.L. Emmet MS, 13417.

117 *G. M. P.,* 182 and also 296.

118 *Ibid.,* 182-83.

119 John Mercer's Ledger, Bucks County Historical Society, Doylestown, Pennsyl-vania.

120 The *Case, loc. cit.,* 31.

121 *Ibid.,* 31.

122 *Journal of Colonel George Washington* . . . Edited, with Notes by J. M. Toner, Albany, N. Y., 1893, 81-82.

123 Historical Society of Pennsylvania, Franklin Papers, Vol. I, Part II, No. 132.

124 *Case* of 1770, *loc. cit.,* 31.

125 *Ibid.,* 33.

126 *Papers of the New Haven Historical Society,* IX, 331-334.

127 *Virginia Magazine of History and Biography,* LX, 412.

128 *G.M.P.,* 209.

129 Memorial of April 11, 1766, *Va. Mag. of Hist. and Biog.,* LX, 412.

130 *Pennsylvania Mag. of Hist. and Biog.,* II, 299-302.

131 *Va. Mag. of Hist. and Biog.,* LX, 412.

132 *Pa. Mag. of Hist. and Biog.,* II, 302.

133 *Md. Arch.,* XIV, 236-237.

134 *Journal of Colonel George Washington,* ed. Toner, I, 87.

135 *Va. Mag. of Hist. and Biog.,* LX, 420.

136 *G.M.P.,* 186.

137 *Ibid.,* 210.

138 Mentioned, *G.M.P.,* 186.

139 *Va. Mag. of Hist. and Biog.,* LX, 406.

140 *Ibid.,* XVII, 325-328.

141 *G.M.P.,* 186.

142 *Ibid.*

143 *Ibid.,* 207.

144 James Mercer Garnett, "James Mercer," *William and Mary Quarterly,* series one, XVII, 89.

145 Rowland, *Mason,* I, 297.

146 *G.M.P.,* 186.

147 Shelburne Papers, L, 93-97.

148 MS., AC 2203, Division of Manuscripts, Library of Congress.

149 *G.M.P.,* 222, 641*n.*

150 *William and Mary Quarterly,* series one, I, 200-203.

151 *G.M.P.,* 221.

152 *Case* of 1770, *loc. cit.,* 34-35.

153 *G.M.P.,* 186-220.

154 *Ibid.,* 221-229.

155 *Ibid.,* 297-310.

156 Letter mentioned, Rowland, *Mason,* I, 133.

157 *Ibid.,* 132-135.

158 *Ibid.,* 136.

159 Samuel Wharton, *Plain Facts* . . . (Philadelphia, 1781), 68-71.

160 P.R.O.C.O. 5: 1332/301-306.

161 *Ibid.,* 1331/307-310.

162 *G.M.P.,* 310.

163 *J.B.T.,* 1768-1775, 159.

164 *Plain Facts,* 149.

165 Mentioned, *G.M.P.*, 311.

166 *Ibid.*, 183.

167 *Ibid.*, 311.

168 Mentioned, *G.W.*, III, 66.

169 See *G.M.P.*, 229.

170 P.R.O.C.O. 5: 1332/365-66.

171 *Ibid.*, 1333/388.

172 *J.B.T.*, 1768-1775, 188.

173 Rowland, *Mason*, I, 151.

174 Mentioned, William Waller Henning, *The Statutes at Large; Being a Collection of All the Laws of Virginia* . . . (11 vols., Richmond, 1875-1893), XII, 366.

175 *Va. Mag. of Hist. and Biog.*, XVIII, 218.

176 *Virginia Gazette*, February 7, 1771.

177 MS., A. L. S., in Arthur Dobbs Papers in North Carolina State Archives, Raleigh, N. C.

178 *Va. Mag. of Hist. and Biog.*, XXII, 326-328.

179 *Ibid.*, XVII, 327-328.

180 Virginia State Library, MS. 20624.

181 Original not found, but seen extensively excerpted in Carter to James Mercer, December 11, 1771.

182 There is much information about this in many deeds of November 1774, made out in Frederick County.

183 *G. W.*, III, 66-70, 72.

184 James Mercer to Robert Carter, December 31, 1771. This letter was once in the possession of Mr. W. Garnett Chisolm, who very kindly gave his permisssion to publish it. Shortly before his death, in 1955, Mr. Chisolm deposited his collection of Garnett and Mercer papers in the Virginia Historical Society.

185 Thomas and Rowland Hume to Robert Carter.

186 *Va. Mag. of Hist. and Biog.*, XVII, 325-328.

187 Tench Tighlman Papers, Maryland Historical Society.

188 *G. W.*, IV, 113-117.

189 *G.M.P.*, 324.

190 *Va. Gazette*, January 14, 1773.

191 Ohio Company Papers of the Etting Collection, Historical Society of Pennsylvania.

192 *G.M.P.*, 512-524, a group of paper forming a veritable James Mercer archive.

193 *Va. Gazette*, September 23, 1773, and October 28, 1773.

194 George Washington to George Mercer, December 1773, in *G. W.*, III, 172, and George Mason to George Washington, December 21, 1773, in *Letters to G. W.*, IV, 286-288.

195 *Va. Mag. of Hist. and Biog.*, XVII, 424.

196 *G. W.*, IV, 286-288.

197 *Ibid.*, III, 197.

198 *Va. Gazette*, June 30, 1774.

199 *Letters to G. W.*, V, 49-50.

200 Robert Carter Papers, Duke University Library.

201 *Letters to G. W.*, V, 61-64.

202 *G. W.*, III, 244.

203 *Virginia Gazette*, November 25, 1773.

204 Library of Congress, Division of Manuscripts Acc 5464.

205 *G. W.*, XXXVII, 507-508.
206 *Ibid.*, III, 249.
207 *Ibid.*, 252-255.
208 *Ibid.*, 283.
209 *Ibid.*, 409.
210 See bond of April 14, 1775, in Ohio Company Papers, in Etting Collection of the Historical Society of Pennsylvania.
211 *G. W.*, III, 401.
212 Mentioned under September 1775, in Treasury I, Bundle 445, folio 136.
213 *Ibid.*, folio 134.
214 *Ibid.*
215 *G.M.P.*, 325.
216 Treasury I, Bundle 445, f. 138.
217 P.R.O.C.O. 5: 154/161.
218 *Ibid.*, 155/40.
219 *G.M.P.*, 326.
220 *Virginia Historical Register*, II (1849), 28.
221 *G. W.*, XVI, 292.
222 Calendar of Franklin Papers, American Philosophical Society, IV, 442.
223 Hening, *Statutes*, XII, 365.
224 *Ibid.*, 366.
225 *Ibid.*, 365.
226 *Ibid.*, 367.
227 *Ibid.*, 368.
228 MS., Virginia State Library.
229 *Diaries of G. W.*, ed. Fitzpatrick, III, 439.
230 *G. W.*, XXX, 190-194.
231 Copies in Virginia Historical Society and in the Alderman Library, University of Virginia.
232 Will Book, Spotsylvania County, Virginia.
233 Deed Book XXVI, 681, Frederick County, Virginia.
234 *Ibid.*
235 MS., Virginia Historical Society.

DATE DUE			
OCT 7 '66			
GAYLORD			PRINTED IN U.S.A.